my dog is a morning person

Snapshots from the life of Kelly Ballard

MY DOG IS A MORNING PERSON

Kelly Ballard

© 2009 by Kelly Ballard. All rights reserved.

ISBN 978-0-578-03099-9

Acknowledgements

I would like to thank my family (Frayne, Dex, Kyle, and Kenny) for being agents of the redemptive process, my in-laws (out at the farm) for almost three decades of home, and my original family (Mom, Dad, Jack, and Mary) for being a part of many memorable experiences from my childhood and youth. I also want to recognize the family of faith of which I'm a part, knowing that we participate in this ongoing journey together. Thank you all.

Forward

I am not entirely unique in letting you know that as I get older, I learn some things about what it means to be humbly grateful. In my younger, ambitious years, I was fairly anxious to arrive, and my imagination conjured the grandeur I thought due me. As I've remembered these following moments of my life, I have come to recognize more and more its wonder. So, I look forward to the years that are waiting to be lived. As you read through these pages, you will see that there's not a lot here about 'successes' and 'accolades' and 'hitting the big note.' Just a bunch of good memories that make me smile and nod.

Hope you do the same!

1
My Dog is a Morning Person

Strange as it may sound, I live on Forest Avenue in Sherwood. You know, as in *Sherwood Forest* in *Robin Hood*. (I, the musician, used to live on Songbird, which was also kind of weird. I've also lived on Newell and Highway 7 and 8th Street and Bradshaw which don't really sound weird at all.) Back to Forest. My house sits on the corner of Forest and Upper Roy (which used to just be Roy until the city decided that there was a Lower Roy that did not connect with Upper Roy so Roy couldn't just be Roy any more. They've also changed all of our house numbers from four digits to five, which is really okay, because our new house number shares both a 1 and a 4 with the old house number, so we only have to buy three new gold numbers for the front of our house, which saves us a bundle.) So, as you've figured out, Roy is a street that runs up a hill—a nice, residential, not-too-often-used street, into which Forest terminates.

Sherwood is Pleasantville. Middle-upper class, safe, clean, and 'perfect' to some.

My house is a simple blockish house. Square. It is gray with dark blue shutters and a red front door. I have the steepest driveway in the history of the world—something I vowed never to have after living with a gently sloping one on Songbird—and a beautiful backyard. The backyard sold me on the house because it has a huge fir tree to which is attached a hammock, a nice lawn—except in the fall when the pine needles fall into a matted mess which chokes it out, lots of shrubs lining the standard 6' fence, a bunny cage for Cookies and Cream (sadly, actually, Cream just died, so it's just Cookies now), and (my favorite) a trickling fountain. (The trickle comes out of the mouth of Ralf the Ceramic Frog—aptly named by my 13-year-old son, Kenny, and me. Ralf, as in: puke, throw-up, or barf. Dad and son together came up, no pun intended, with that one.) We also have a big metal eagle named Isaiah (that used to sit glued to the top of a wooden light pole to which one end of the hammock was attached (insufficiently, so that when it jerked loose of the pole and dropped 18-year-old, 6'1" second son Kyle to the ground, Isaiah came tumbling down to the ground, but not onto Kyle, fortunately), and a red ceramic eagle inside the dining room named Jeremiah. We have a mallard decoy floating in the trickling pond that has not been named.

We also have a dog. Her name is Sierra. (Oh, I was just informed that Sierra chewed up the mallard, so that's one less thing we have to name, unless we just name it Gone. That reminds me of two fish we had in the little trickling pond thingie. Sierra ate one of them, and we called the other one Fortunate, until it died mysteriously.)

Sierra is a morning person.

Except for me, Sierra is the only other morning person in the house. I suppose, that in addition to the eagles and frogs and all that, I should introduce you to the night owls. Dex(ter) is the oldest of three children. He is a college junior. He is about 6'1" 260, with blonde hair. He is solid. He is built. He has always been that way. (Not that tall always, because you would have heard about that by now—a baby born like that, but built big and solid.) He's solid in a lot of other ways too. I'm proud of him. Kyle may be just a little bit smaller than Dex, but that doesn't mean he's small, and he just finished up his senior year of high school. He's solid in a lot of ways also, not the least of which is the fact that he worked his junior year as a banker. My banker son. Go figure. He worked (up until football drew him away) at his own window and handed out lots of money to rich people. "Dad, I saw $40,000 today!" said he on his first day at work. Kenny is in seventh grade, wiry, quick, a lover of baseball and geography (the school champ at Archer Glen, and a fierce competitor at State, mind you.) You'll be hearing more about these three later.

Then there is my wife, Frayne, whom you'll get to know as well. But for now, suffice it to say that she is the life of the party and the happiest part of our lives.

Oh, and me. Sorry about that. I'm just a regular middle-aged, middle-class American Christian guy. I do the music and leadership thing in a church and do some other gigging and speaking and travel now and then, and I'm not famous or well known. I like myself an awful lot, but I don't think I'm all *that* conceited.

We're a pretty good family overall.

For the first year and a half of her life, Sierra slept in the laundry room where she belongs. Even though I call her a morning person, she's really *not* a human. She's a regular old dog, daresay I, a mutt. She is part Australian Shepherd and part, um, let's see, what is she? I think that would be Lab. I don't know. She is medium in size, with a reddish, shortish-long coat and these weird tawny eyes. I'm not sure what tawny means, but that's what I think they are. Now that Sierra is older and can be expected to act responsibly, she has graduated to sleeping on Kyle's floor. (She was his

Christmas present one year...which sort of surprised him, because he was hoping for a Husky or a Malamute, and she looked more like a rat coming straight from the pound.) They love each other though. Also, she really loves Kenny and has even graduated to sleeping *on his bed*, which is the top bunk, and she uses his office chair to jump on up there.

I'm usually the first one up in the morning, and when Sierra hears me, she scritch-scratches on either door of either room until I come and let her out. She at that point is ready for a transitory excursion. We can't say 'walk' anymore, because she goes freakazoid ballistic, and we can't spell W-A-L-K, because she goes freakazoid ballistic, and we can't even say 'W' anymore because, well, you know...

We try to take her up to the ball park and throw either the tennis ball or a racquetball or a Frisbee-which I like the best except for the fact that it gets the slobberiest. But, she likes to run and jump and catch and come back and drop it and sit and wag and foam at the mouth, and that makes for a pretty good dog.

This reminds me of our other not so pretty good dog, Kujo.

Actually, her name was Ivy. We got her as a Christmas present for Kyle when he was around four. (We might as well have gotten him a set of butcher knives or sulfuric acid.) Ivy was a German Shepherd (and I mean that, *was*...which probably has you wondering what she is now, like a Pekinese or a Poodle or something less destructive like a Schnauzer. But actually, she's found her way six feet under in Grandma and Grandpa's horse pasture out at the farm, which is pretty sad, and which is also the end of my Ivy story, which I'll get to in a minute.) So a guy that we knew gave us Ivy, because, he said, "Every boy needs a dog," which, referring to a dog like Ivy translates into, "Every boy needs a severe, life-threatening danger in his life." It was such a sweet gesture, and ah, gee shucks, how could we say no? Ivy was the 'pick of the litter' which really makes me wonder what the other cute little Kujos must have turned out like. I took her home, and we did all the things we were supposed to do to train her, (things I learned raising 101 Dalmatians and Papillons when I was a kid), and all was going great until she was about, oh, six months old.

Then, it happened. Something traumatized her and she was never the same again.

Our home was in the mountains of Colorado at the time, in the shadow of Longs Peak at 9200', (I now digress, because I can't not mention the spectacular beauty and grandeur of that place where we were fortunate to live for a time.) On our property was located a small plake (which is smaller than a lake and bigger than a pond), at which we fished and swam in the sunshine and ice skated in the winter, which does make a lot of sense, because in the winter it's more frozen than the rest of the year. (We lived at a camp, actually, and one time, we had this winter junior high retreat, and we were trying to think of a big splash—no pun intended—entrance for me, the host of the thing, and so I put on my Hawaiian swim trunks and spiked my hair—when I had it—purple, and put on a couple of snow skis, and in 19 degree weather, I 'water skied' behind a snow machine across said frozen plake, and that was pretty funny and memorable.) The other memorable thing about that plake and Ivy in the winter, is (a) how Kyle accidentally ice skated over Ivy's tail and cut it off, and she sprayed significant blood speckles all over the ice as she howled and wagged, which seemed incongruent to me, and (b) how we built an 8X8 warming shed complete with benches and a wood stove, and we were in there once during a storm, and the wind huffed and it puffed so hard, that it blew that shed down with us and fire all inside of it, but Ivy escaped, and that little doggie ran wee wee wee all the way home, and since one of the guys in there was our maintenance guy who was wearing a hat, the worst thing for Ivy from that day on was cowboys because they wear big hats…except cowboys in ice skates, which really messes her up.

    But she was a really good dog with us around home…she could keep her Inner Puppy in check—probably, because we didn't wear our cowboy hats and ice skates around the house. Good call on that one, for a lot of reasons. Anyway, I put the little fear biter down one day, and I put her deceased body in the Hefty bag and drove her out in the Suburban to the farm, and there she lays, right next to my sister-in-law's horse who maybe was a fear kicker or something.

    This all sadly reminds me of when my folks gave away my Dalmatian named Polly, when I think she actually got put to sleep, and how much both the death of the dog and the confusion over the truth of it all broke my tender 13-year-old heart. I guess this is why it is pretty heartwarming that after Frisbee, Sierra and I return home, and I eat oatmeal (when I'm good), or sausage and eggs (when I'm bad), or sausage and eggs and an Eggo or two (when I'm quite bad), and she wanders around my feet keeping me company and begging for attention and food like a good morning person ought to, and I know we're going to hang on to her for awhile, and our lives are better for it.

Well, this is all good, so I think that tomorrow morning, Sierra and I will get up and go for another (I have to whissssper now) T-R-A-N-S-I-T-O-R-Y E-X-C-U-R-S-I-O-N.

2
My Friends Are Funny

There's nothing like a great bout of side-splitting laughter with funny friends, as long as they're laughing *with* me, not *at* me.

The first great laughter memory that comes immediately to mind happened during my junior year of high school in Anacortes, Washington, which I think is the prettiest town I've ever been to, except maybe Winnemucca in August (just kidding about the August part.) Anacortes is the 'gateway to the San Juan Islands,' the most invigorating and life-giving archipelago that I've ever been to. (I haven't been to many archipelagos, now that I think about it, and I wonder if they really are supposed to be invigorating and life-giving, but if I were an archipelago, I would sure want to be referred to as invigorating and life-giving rather than mundane and energy-sucking. I mean, if you're going to be an archipelago you might as well offer something beautiful...) If you're wondering what an archipelago is, just picture this particular archipelago as islands of varying sizes and shapes occupying the 100-mile saltwater stretch between Olympia in the south and the Straight of Juan de Fuca in the north—the straight that separates the Olympic Peninsula from the south shore of Vancouver Island.

Where was I? Oh yeah...Anacortes.

The other thing I like about Anacortes (other than Village Pizza on Commercial where virtually every last high-schooler-one-of-us went on Fridays after the game and where my brother worked after he graduated, and I remember him wrecking his white 1963 Corvair coupe with the red interior about that same time, but now I'm off on some kind of a rabbit trail which is where I think he might have been out east of town) is that it is one of those great places where the mountains really do meet the sea. The Canadian Cascades are to the north, the Olympic Mountains lie to the southwest, and Mt. Baker looms large to the east. Mt. Erie (really, more like a little molehill—I want to use the word 'tit' right there because it is so descriptive, but I'm afraid of my female friends and female enemies and my Christian friends and enemies that I don't know I have—than anything else) sticks up to the close south and is home to all kinds of crazy people who like to trust their lives to ropes. (Oh, I should mention that rock climbing is one of my favorite sports, which makes me....yeah, crazy.)*

Anacortes has lots of craggy rocks and pebbly shores and a little bit of sand and kelp. Not quite Hawaiian, but it has beaches. And orcas. And bald eagles. And salmon. Fishing boats and crabbing boats and fishermen and crab fishermen (which really help make the boats a lot more effective than if they didn't exist at all).

And basketball.

Anacortes basketball. Now, I tried out for this basketball team and definitely would have made it except for small-town politics. (But I'm over it.) No, actually, I just wasn't very good. There was a skinny kid who said he was my friend (and grew up there in Anacortes, which I didn't), and another kid who was really good (who grew up there in Anacortes, which I didn't), and the kid with the Italian name (who grew up there in Anacortes, which I didn't), and the stocky one who smoked marijuana, I think (who grew up there in Anacortes, which I didn't); and they all made the team, and I didn't. As if growing up there in Anacortes really makes a difference. (But I'm over it.) Had I made the team there in Anacortes, though, I would not have lived the story I am now telling, so it's all good. However, if I had made the team there in Anacortes (which may have happened if I had grown up there), then I would probably be telling a different story about how I hit the game-winning shot in the WSAA 2A State Championship game of 1979 and then had my name in the Seattle PI and the Seattle Times and would have become famous and notorietied and landed a scholarship right out of high school and then played for the Supersonics, but that sounds like a pretty boring story compared to my story.

Since I was not to be out on the floor on this particular Friday night against the Ferndale Eagles (oh, we were the Seahawks, and we wore purple), I went about considering with Ken Witter and Don Macy what sort of immature and goofy shenanigans we might undertake at said basketball game.

See, if I wasn't going to be a great basketball star for Anacortes High School, and choir boys were considered faggots (the wrestlers' word, not mine); I needed to find other ways to become popular, which is all that mattered to any of us back then. So, third in line past athletics and music was my terrific sense of humor and mostly unintentional ability to make people laugh—always with me, not at me, of course. It didn't hurt that Ken and Don were already popular (both happened to have a good mix of athleticism, music, and sense of humor—well-rounded, just like me!) Ken was a local DJ at age 15, and Don had a great build (nice biceps, I remember) and was the quintessential star running back on the football team, which I also could have been if I had grown up there in Anacortes, not to mention the great build and biceps. (But I'm over it.)

Our plan worked on that Friday night, and the notoriety of which I wrote was instantly granted. Radio and all.

I might remind you that 'streaking' was at its zenith during these years. (Again, my female and Christian friends and male friends, too, are squirming at this visual.)

Not wanting to do serious time in the Anacortes jail, we put on boxers and ski masks (nothing else except towels around our waists) and waited until halftime before 'streaking' out in a speedy blaze of energy from one corner of the basketball court to the other diagonal corner and out the double doors to the parking lot, past our cars, over an embankment, into the gully behind the school where no one could find us! It was there that we laughed and laughed and made ourselves proud of our wonderful accomplishment, just knowing that all of those Seahawk fans—every last one of them—were interrupting their popcorn runs asking the question, "Who were those masked men?!"

Now that I think about it, I'm getting my stories mixed up, because the one I wanted to tell was about how Ken and Don and I were hanging out in the locker room during the first half of a Seahawk basketball game, and we were fully clothed, and Don told a (sort of dirty) joke, and we started laughing, and we laughed so hard that it bred deeper laughter, and eye contact fed the breeding of more laughter and—I kid you not—we laughed all the way through the first half and into the third quarter before we picked ourselves up off the benches and floors and composed ourselves and quieted to silly girl giggles and then to intermittent guffaws and then smiles all around before we could actually go get our own popcorn.

* * *

The other great laugh I remember happened just a few years later on the eastern flank of Oregon State's signature peak, Mt. Hood.

If Anacortes is first on my list, then eastern Multnomah County is a close second. Whereas Anacortes is the 'gateway to the San Juan Islands,' EMC (I just made that up) is the gateway to both the northern Oregon Cascade Mountains and the Columbia River Gorge. The OCM and the CRG (I just made those up) connect right there in EMC.

I was living in Gresham, newly married and working for a church directing its choir and cleaning its toilets. In return, I was given a dinky little puny (noted and intended redundancies) three bedroom and $500 a month. Wow. At age 22, I actually had my own home and a salary and a bunch of church people who seemed to like me and a 21-year-old beauty that I got to sleep with every night.

And a '65 Chevy pickup.

Life was good! Oh so good!

One of the guys in the church had made a fireplace insert in metal shop and had given it to the church to put in this dinky little puny (DLP) house. So we heated that DLP house almost exclusively with firewood. I can see that you're doing the math already: wood stove needs wood, man of house has truck, Oregon forests abound directly east of DLP. You're on to something here…

My friend Dwain also needed firewood, and since we were both in our early twenties and driving trucks and running noisy and heavy things like chain saws made our biceps bulge like Don Macy's, we decided to set apart a Saturday for a wood-getting, male-bonding venture.

Not that it's entirely important, but a little more on the truck now.

If I were to run a want ad describing said truck, it might look something like this:

1965 Chevy ½ Ton

white, wood bed, runs well

could use some cosmetic care, but not bad

make offer

What wouldn't go in the ad is all the information about what little things make such a truck difficult to drive. It had no power steering, of course, but it did have a little red one of those thing-a-ma-jiggers that you steer with—that little handle thing that spins in one hand, which is entirely necessary when you're shifting the 'three on the tree' gear shift. Now, all of that isn't so bad, except this particular truck had no turn signal switch, so you had to use your left arm out the window for that, which leaves you one arm short—especially if you're turning onto Lombard Street in San Francisco, which I never had to do in that particular truck, because I never drove it farther than the eastern flank of Oregon's signature peak.

So Dwain and I put our (huge) chain saws in the back of the truck, along with the accompanying wood-cutting accoutrement like boots and axes and plaid shirt-jackets and Stihl hats, not to mention lunches and appropriate libation. Being a choir-directing janitor and all, and him being a seminary student and all, we decided to leave the Copenhagen and the Playboys back at the DLP. (Just kidding, female and Christian friends.)

After smoking our way (the truck, not us) up past 4000', we found a little logging road just past Mt. Hood Meadows, still shining in the morning sunlight. We followed that for a few miles and found just the perfect woodcutting ravine. Here's what I don't understand. Why aren't fallen trees ever laying across the roadway except when you don't really want them to be, like when you're driving out to the coast to go crabbing and a windstorm comes through the Oregon Coast Range (OCR) and 30,000,000 trees all fall across Highway 26? But, when you're woodcutting, then, oh no, they have to have fallen sixty plus feet down a fern and nettle-thick forest in the mud. But, being two tough Oregon guys with boots and axes and plaid shirt-jackets and Stihl hats and machetes and bulldozers and Napalm and tracking guides and helicopters, we would be just fine.

So we cut up one of those trees—probably a fir, though it might have been a pine. It was tall and had a trunk and some green things that were needles, but maybe not…and I know it wasn't a cedar, because I know the smell of cedar from putting a roof of cedar shakes on a house when I was a kid.

But rather than cut up one of those trees in fireplace-length logs, we cut it up in sections that were about six or eight feet long for the purpose of expedient extraction. Then, being two tough Oregon guys with boots and all, we each crouched at our respective ends of one particular log and muscularly lifted that log off of the muddy fern-ground up about as high as we could get it, which was, oh, about a millimeter. But then we really put our backs into it and got it up to about crotch-high before struggling to scootch ourselves back up the slippery ravine. We scootched and rested and then scootched some more—soon thoroughly exhausted after about ten minutes of scootching (try scootching up a big muddy ravine carrying something far too heavy in an attempt to prove your Oregon manliness, and you'll know what I mean when I say we weren't making very much progress.) Oh, one other thing I should mention. We weren't going side-by-side up the hill. Dwain was backing up the hill, the log pointed downhill to where I was bearing the brunt of the weight. (I guess we now know who the toughest Oregon guy of the two was.)

We started to chuckle as we scootched.

Then, when Dwain's heavy boot-clad feet slipped out from under him, and he landed flat on his big Oregon behind in the mud-fern guck, we began to chortle.

We stood and strained and lifted and began to scootch some more.

Then, we flat-out howled when he slipped and butt-sat again!

But then, I really, really began to laugh uncontrollably, which made Dwain laugh uncontrollably. He thought I was laughing uncontrollably because we were two tough Oregon guys looking absolutely out of control and foolish.

I laughed at least ten interrupted minutes of the absolute deepest, most painful, tear-jerking belly laugh I had ever laughed (even more than in an Anacortes locker room), because Dwain was unaware of the fact that upon the third time of slippage, his splaying legs had just put too much tension on his 501's, which split all the way from zipper to backside in one quick r-r-r-r-rip! There he was with his tighty-whiteys completely exposed and his big Oregon boy smile and laughter proving his oblivion and innocence all in one beautiful picture of side-splitting *and* pants-splitting drama!

*Rock climbing is really safe as long as you do everything correctly and your gear holds out. Otherwise, you will probably 'divot'**, and that's not good. I've never had that experience, and I've never helped anyone else ever have that experience, though I do remember a time or two when I La-La-Landed out when I was belaying, but Thomas or Jack or Whomever stayed close to the rock and never knew the difference. I've only been nervous twice— once on my first climb, when, sitting on a little ledge about eighty feet up, Thomas said, "Just hook yourself into that little metal loop sticking out of the rock over there and swing out on your rope." Um, yeah. And the other time was the night before Kenny was born, and I asked myself that TRCQ (taboo rock climbing question): "Why the hell am I doing this again, and what would happen if that broke or he screwed up or weather came in or even meteors struck or I had a heart attack or got a runny nose and…?" as I was making a crux move about two hundred feet off the ground.

**divot: to put a big hole in the ground with your body, most effectively accomplished by falling from a significant height.

3

My Boat is Inspiring

Okay, so now I'm going to tell you about my funny little boat. But first let me tell you why my boat is a life-giving, inspiring, funny little boat, starting with the little part.

It's little because it's only sixteen feet (15'-8" actually) long. It's funny because it's old old old. Her name is Gertrude. (I really don't want anyone to be offended that I chose this name. I can't remember why I call her that, except it sounds geriatric and that probably makes you upset if you are named Gertrude, and for that I am profoundly and sincerely sorry. It's even worse if you're 19 and some consider you a hottie and your name is Gertrude, but I am having a hard time picturing that, but you never know.) You can look this up on the Internet (not ladies named Gertrude, but the type of boat she is) to get a picture. 1978 Glastron TS 158. Orange. Tri-hull. She's got a 1978 Johnson outboard motor on her stern (which is better than on the bow, which would make it a really funny little boat!) that actually has enough power to pull my 200+ pound young men sons out of the water. I think people laugh at my boat, but I'm not sure. Actually, yeah, they do. The people who laugh are not 45. They are 25 and are cut and bronze and T & A and loud and have lots and lots of money and have brand new wakeboard boats that cost $50,000 or $60,000 or in the millions and they have wakeboard towers and sound systems and motors that are bigger than mine. They also have lots of beer and sexy accoutrement that come with these boats and they look like they're having lots of fun laughing at me, if that's why they're laughing. (I wouldn't blame them for laughing, actually, because like I said, my boat is little AND funny and I can own that.)

Now the life-giving part and I really mean this.

When I was a kid we had enough money for fancy ski boats (Glastrons) that came with everything but the beer and women (those were extras that my parents didn't spring for, which always kind of bummed me out because I always thought, "Hey, if you're going to drop that kind of dime on a family time investment, you might as well not just settle for the fish-finder, if you know what I mean.") I didn't always think that, really, but now when I think it it's kind of funny, so it made it in here.

I want to describe these Glastrons, and then tell one quick story that just pops into my head about boats and beer and women, and then I'll get back to the live-giving, funny little boat story.

Glastron #1 came to us early in the '70's. It was a 21-foot tri-hull that my dad called the Mari Mari. My mom's name is Marilyn and my sister's name is Mary. I'm pretty sure I'm getting it right when I say there's a connection there. Or maybe the little line on the left side of the 'h' was not high enough, so the 'h's turned into 'r's and the boat was really the Mahi Mahi in honor of our dolphin friends or something. (All of this reminds me of when I was on a TV show in 4th grade and the producer of the show wrote 'Mary Christmas' on the screen and I said, "Hey, you spelled 'merry' wrong," so he went back and "fixed" it: 'Marry Christmas.' I have wondered about TV producers ever since.) The Mari Mari also had a cuddy and so the five of us in the family could go boat camping and all stay dry, for there were two bunks up in the cuddy (the place below the forward deck) as well as two back-to-back seat sets that folded into bunks and then the floor between there where my sister, Mary, should have slept because she was the smallest, but I usually ended up there because we did not want Mary to not be merry. (Her middle name is Chris and I've always thought it would have been funny if she had married a guy with the last name Moss because then she would have been Mary Chris Moss (or Marry Chris Moss, if you're a TV producer), but she married a guy named Gifford, which doesn't seem that remarkable to me.

Glastron #2 came to us a couple of years after Glastron #1. (We traded the Mari Mari in on the Mari Mari II, a very original name, I think. I can still remember in my nostrils the smell of fiberglass boat stores in Los Gatos, where we kids would wait and wait and wait with droopy eyes while my mom and dad picked out colors. Royal blue and white, in case you were wondering.) Mari Mari II was Dad's pride and joy because not only did she have the beef of the Mari Mari engine, but she was a V-hull and three feet shorter, which made her slice through the water faster than most 'haystacks' out there.

For a stretch of a few good years there we did our share of fishing and skiing with those two boats. Our favorite destination, by far, was Clair Engle Lake (Lake Trinity), nestled in the bosom (another interesting and descriptive word choice) of the Trinity Alps in Northern California. While everyone else from the Bay Area seemed satisfied with the larger and closer Lake Shasta, we pulled the Mari Maris up the extra miles past Whiskeytown Reservoir, in a winding road serpentine to our favorite Trinity launches, behind our royal blue and white 1972 GMC Sierra camper-laden three quarter ton, gladly singing Donna Fargo tunes while listening to KRAK.

The most notable of these trips (except for the one where I accidentally poured a pitcher of lemonade all over the back of the brand new Mari Mari II engine hatch and stern seats and I can still hear the Trinity canyon reverberations of my dad's tongue-lashing or the one at what we called 'Butterfly Cove' where the tiger swallowtails landed on my head and shoulders and fingers and just stayed there) happened during my twelfth year. It was what we called a 'boys trip' and Marilyn and Mary were left home, excluded. Dad, Jack and I got a campsite at Trinity and were pleased and even thrilled to have no neighbors throughout the entire campground…until…*they* drove in, 'they' meaning a bona fide, actual, legitimate, hog-straddling, beer-drinking, women-toting group of some of the meanest-looking, loudest, obnoxious Hells Angels that California could ever hope to put forth. I think you've got them pictured.

Fortunately, they chose sites about three or four separated from us, so it wasn't awful to have them there. They seemed to honor the 11:00 quiet hour and we didn't have to have much to do with them. At first.

Third day in I think it was, the three of us woke up early—way pre-dawn—and put together our fishing day's needs: food, clothing, gear. We locked up our belongings, took valuables with us, and walked to the edge of the ravine, the trail of which led to the mooring of the Mari Mari II, fifty-some feet below us. Jack and Dad went on ahead, as for some reason I was delayed slightly. I think I remember it this way: From the trail down below came running brother Jack with a pretty shocked look on his face, as in, "Dad has been apprehended by blood-sucking aliens and you need to run and get help." Actually he simply reported to me that Dad had fallen and severely broken his ankle and I, little brother, was the only one who could go and get help.

Yeah, right.

As a pre-pubescent pimply-faced scrawny little blonde kid who was just beginning to come into his interested-in-girls-more-than-trout phase, I couldn't help but transport myself into the following thought: 'Maybe the entire cheerleading squad from Santa Clara University is finally here and they can pitch in. Surely they like camping. Surely they come out here on their own. Surely they would be willing to help, as well as comfort me in my time of need.' But a motley crew of hung over bikers was the closest second I could think of, so off I went.

To make a long story short (I haven't forgotten that this story is just a precursor to the Gertrude story), the Angels of Hell were gracious and kind and acted in a very Christian manner, climbing down the ravine, hoisting 240 pound Dad up on their shoulders, carrying him up the ravine, putting him in a rusty and rust colored 1960-something Olds Cutlass, driving him down the serpentine road to the Redding hospital, sitting with him while the professionals put him in a cast, dragging him back up the highway to the campground, and each and every one of them signing his foot-to-hip cast with suggestive and otherwise inappropriate autographs, which I, as a pre-pubescent pimply faced scrawny little blonde kid thoroughly appreciated, as I still had Kate and Jenny and Laurie and Kim and Jacque and the rest of the Santa Clara Cheer Squad pictured clearly in my mind.

So that's that.

One down side to the Mari Maris is the fact that for some reason I was never allowed to drive them. (Maybe it was the whole cheerleader thing my dad was afraid of, that my mind wouldn't be fully on the task or something.) I always wondered why a guy would have a boat and not ever let his kids drive it. So I grew up with this idea that I would never be worthy of taking steering and power in hand and pouring on the coals or giving it the mustard (not real mustard, given the lemonade debacle) or whatever you want to call it. Or maybe it had to do with submerged tree trunks and other boats (which are good to look out for) or capsizing potential or waves or lightning or sea monsters or something. I don't know. I just don't know. I just don't know what the deal was with all of that unwillingness to share and share alike.

But here's what I do know. I am now the dad and I have the Glastron and I can do whatever I dang well please with it.

There are two choices for us here in Oregon. We can drive an hour or two and be at some of the prettiest mountain lakes around, or we can pull out of our driveway, get gas at the Newberg Chevron, and put in on the Willamette, just below the stinky mill. It should be mentioned that the Willamette is not quite Chernobyl, but it's getting close. We swim and ski in it from time to time, because it's nearby, but that makes us really on the lookout for kids that glow in the dark and puke up their guts and stuff like that—which can be sort of the down side of a day of water sports.

We rather choose to go on up into Washington state, right in the shadow of Mt. St. Helens, which shouldn't erupt for about another 3,000 years, which makes us feel relatively safe, compared to the Willnobyl.

The second time we took this new old boat out to the lake was with a couple of other family friends. After launching and sputter-starting the ol' gal up, a few of us loaded her down with tube and skis and lunch and dog and bar-b-q and towels and sunscreen and ropes and ladder and chain saws and tents and ping pong table and pool table and foosball table and hot tub (no, just kidding)…a whole bunch of stuff in order to go out and try to find a suitable place to picnic (or spend the rest of our lives, which we could easily have done with all that we loaded Gertrude up with.) After finding the great beach, we dropped stuff and people and went back to shuttle the others the fifteen minute ride back. We then spent the day doing what you do at the lake, which really consists of drinking a lot of (lake) water due to water-ski-face-plants, and eating too much and getting sunburned and really, really tired. Actually, next to mountain climbing and basketball, water skiing is my favorite athletic activity. There's something about glasswater and warmth and cutting hard that brings a real and literal smile to my face. There are always the spills and chills, like the time I took a nose dive back in the day and the old ski ring I was wearing around my waste schwooped off my body, taking my swim suit with it. Fortunately my ankles caught the lining of the suit and I could dog paddle long enough to pull them back up before Mom and Mary and Aunt Lori came a-swinging back around in the boat. But all in all, skiing is pure joy to me.

At the end of this particularly wonderful experience (not the losing of the suit…I'm back at the Mt. St. Helens lake now), knowing we were low on gas, and room, we began the shuttle back. Frayne and I got out at the dock, and there, sitting behind the steering wheel was my son, Dex, with those big eyes saying, 'I'll go back and get the others.' Dex, the one who had only piloted Gertrude one or two times, of course, made me think twice.

And then a childhood history of never getting to drive the Glastrons hit me between the eyes like a boat paddle and I released the line on the dock, thus releasing my son from the boundaries imposed on me when I was him, pushed the bow to the south-southeast and watched the boy in the boat drive away in a tumultuous flurry of wave, wake, wind and not just a little bit of emanating fatherly joy.

I'd rename her Redemption, but maybe that will just be a good name for the next one, rather than just regular old Gertrude II.

4
My Sport is Basketball

I had quite a wonderful career out on the baseball diamond.

That's not entirely accurate.

I played softball twice.

The first time was when I was in fourth grade, and I played right field, (I know, go ahead and say it), for Kyle Realty. I barely remember it, but I do recall that it had its boring elements.

The second time was for a fast-pitch team at my church—the same one in EMC. After being cut from the Anacortes basketball team, I wasn't thrilled when I heard the coach of this church league team say, (rather snottily and snootily), "Well, we really don't have enough jerseys for someone like you." (Maybe if I'd grown up in EMC, but I'm over it.) But I played anyway—not because I was stubborn, but because I was stupid.

I had a lousy glove, but I could hit poorly. (That reminds me of a time when we were painting our new house one day, and it was going painfully and arduously slooooowly, and we decided our motto should be: WE'RE SLOW, BUT WE'RE SLOPPY. Same kind of deal here with the baseball, uh, I mean softball thing.)

I had my share of errors, but my hitting flat sucked. The only time I made contact was when I hit this incredible fly ball out over the left fielder's head. Unfortunately, two things went wrong with that one and only hit: 1) It was foul. 2) I forgot to hold onto the bat which easily cleared the third baseman. I was quite the talk of the town for a long time after that which made me proud!

Football was not so great either. Remember I told you that I was kind of scrawny? I didn't have the Don Macy build. I played for the LaConner Braves my sophomore year. (The Native Americans of the Swinomish tribe didn't like me very much, which I can't understand. In fact, one time during halftime of a basketball game, they switched my underwear with the underwear of one of their own that they didn't like, and then they all laughed when we showered and got dressed. Took me a few days to figure out why, when I finally recognized the waist logo was not my standard Fruit of the Loom—not that I wore them for three days, mind you, but upon retrieving them from the dryer. Rest easy on that one. It's actually cool that that happened, because now when I don't care for someone, I just switch his underwear with someone else's, and I feel a lot better.) I wasn't a very confident football player at LaConner partly because of how I felt I was viewed, and partly because I'd never played before, and partly because my talent level was akin to a fourth-grade softball player in right field. One other thing about that: I was kind of afraid to hit or get hit, and that's probably a detriment in that particular sport. I then played at Anacortes for a few games my junior year. My claim to fame was that I picked up a blocked punt and started running with it. That was the good news, but all of my sports stories have an unfortunate side, and this one contained that fact that the only player I had to beat to score was the punter and, um, he caught me and tackled me, and so that's that. My football career ended a few games later when I got steamrollered, flattened, blocked, whatever you want to call it, (Thumped? Obliterated? Murdered?), by a running back on a Student Body Left. I felt like I got hit by the freshman class, the sophomore class, the junior class, the senior class, the Army, Air Force, Coast Guard, Navy and Marines. I only remember lying on the field looking at the sideline thinking, "There's got to be a way to get from here to there." Pops was just standing there shaking his head…and I think he was thinking, "I hope if and when he gets over here, he won't come over to me, because he looks absolutely shameful."

I don't want to mention golf. Or bowling.

No, actually, a quick little word on golf here: I once played in a tournament, and out of 120 guys, I was 119, and all of our names got displayed up on this big reader board thing, and that was pretty embarrassing. If I had just had three more strokes, I would have beat out the biggest golfing loser of the day and won free golf lessons, but as it turned out, I didn't go home with anything but a little prime rib in my belly and, well, that's about it.

I play a little basketball now, which I'm pretty sure I couldn't live without.

I do have some elevation issues, and I'm not talking about Longs Peak and 9200'. Yes, I'm talking about my vertical. For those of you who don't know, a baller's vertical is that distance between the floor and the soles of his Nikes at the top of his jump. So, the really good, good rebounders and dunkers are the ones with, obviously, the greatest vertical—the ones that jump, and you could drive a Hummer underneath. They suspend. They fly. I stick. I slide. My vertical is, uh, ahem, well, when I jump, you could probably slide a razor blade underneath. So, that's a bit of an issue.

I have another issue. Here it is: I play with guys who are 1/3 my age. Or at least 1/2 my age. This is why it's an issue: They never tire. They never rest. They never slow down. And they don't have hair on their backs. And, here's the kicker, *they stay dry*. Whereas these guys can go out and play full court basketball for two hours and never break a sweat, I begin to perspire right at the moment that I bend over to tie up my high tops. That's another thing that gets me! I have to wear high tops and two pairs of socks, (been doing that since 1974—years and years before most of these guys were born!), and on top of that, I wear two ankle braces—one for each ankle, you see. These guys wear these cute little running socks and these nifty little low top shoes...How do they do that?! I do not, however, wear a headband or wristband or geeky goggles, and my shorts are long and saggy, which is boss-groovy-hip, and I don't wear roadkill t-shirts. But, whatever I do wear is soaked through after one fast break and defensive stand. So be it. I think chicks dig me when I'm sweaty—especially when I go shirtless, and they can see my hairy back, which complements my bald head.

So my basketball motto is, "I can't jump, but I sweat profusely."

So many grand b-ball memories come to mind, that I don't know where to start. Let's just say, that I am obsessed and crazed by the playing of this sport. There is nothing better than hitting the game-winner when it's tied, or coming from behind, or hitting the long court pass to the streaking (don't go there) release man, or really getting elevation on a jump shot (not sure what that feels like, really), or saving a ball that's going out of bounds by leaping (not sure what that's like), or soaring for a put back rebound (not sure what that's like), or hearing the squeaky sound of shoes on wood floor, the tweeting of the whistle, that hollow basketball bouncing sound, the lights, the bands, the TV cameras, the cheerleaders (not sure what that's like)…

One day, I just couldn't wait to get out there and play! I had invited Kyle to come play with us at the church, where we, incidentally, have a wood floor, which is better than the tile or carpet floors that come in most churches. For purists like myself, the tile ones are just ugly and slippery and stupid, and the carpet ones don't allow for the hearing of that hollow basketball bouncing sound. And I hate to be late, because then I don't get into the first game, and I hate waiting for the second game. (Patience and basketball aren't good bedfellows. Where did that word come from? That seems like a weird one.) So, I had it timed out perfectly that I would run and get my new Nikes from the store at the mall and meet Kyle there at the same time, so we could then ride together and show up at the church at 3:30 sharp! But, of course, there was traffic, as if everyone from EMC came over to the West Side where I live and decided to get basketball shoes all on the same day. But get there I did, and try on shoes I did, and hook up with Kyle I did, but time kept on slippin' slippin' slippin' into the future (doot doot doo doot), and before I knew it, I realized that, though I had my shoes in hand (after three separate stores and gifts cards and credit cards and all that), I was going to get back on the road at 3:32, which meant that I wasn't going to be able to make the 12-minute drive in minus 2 minutes, and I would be (gasp!) late for the first game! But no worries! I made the 12-minute drive (all the time with young Kyle watching my every exemplary driving moves, which reminds me of how stupid I can really be) in about

0:8:32, which meant I'd make it for at least the second round of the pretty-average-church-pick-up-league draft.

To the locker room I speedily and breathlessly ran!

I opened my shoe box! There they were, right where I left them, spooned together in a footwear embrace!

I put on my first pair of socks—inside out, blue striped! I put on my second pair of socks—right side in and stripeless white!

I tightly laced up each ankle brace on left foot and right!

Into the deep of the first shoe I reached and removed the tissue-ish brown paper! Onto the left foot I placed that shoe, snug and comfy! (I am going to fly today, thought I, really soar!)

Into the deep of the other shoe I reached and removed the tissue-ish brown paper! And then, (you're not gonna believe this!)...IT WAS ANOTHER LEFT SHOE!

Now what am I doing here sitting at the computer?! I have since returned that left right shoe, and certainly some young guys are waiting for a sweaty old guy to show up to make it five on five just about right now.

Can't wait...and I'm grateful for my life and my health and the chance for just a couple more times up and down the court.

5
My Kids are Incredulous

I have tried to be a good dad.

I was just telling someone today about Flip-Around-Thingie. That's a good and sweet memory. When Dex and Kyle were just little fellers, I would come home from work, and they would yell, "Fwip awound fingie! Fwip awound fingie!" So I would fwo duh bweefcase on the fwoor (that makes me sound like Ward, as in Ward Cleaver, doesn't it, coming home with a briefcase?), and Frayne would come out in her big hair and high heels (no, just kidding—I wouldn't wish that on anyone), and I'd lie down on my back on the floor, my knees bent, and flat-floor feet pointing to the Little Fellers all the way across the living room.

First came Kyle, (who was really a cute kid, except for the one day I was leaving to go to work and picked up said bweefcase and turned the door knob, and he looked up at me and said, "See ya' shithead," which, of course stunned the you-know-what out of me, because we don't talk like that at our house, so I said, "What did you say?" and he said, "See ya' shithead," again, and I just kept turning that ol' door knob and was on my way. Yes, just like the Cleavers, golly gee. Kyle also couldn't really say the 'S' sound very well, so he would come up with things like, "I'm putting on my hooze and hocks," and, "I'm going to get you with my hord." That was pretty cute.) So he would run across the floor at full speed and land his little bum right on the tops of my feet, while I would grab his little patties (hands) and thrust my feet upward. This of course, would send him ass-over-tea-kettle, flipping over me (hence Flip-Around-Thingie) and landing on his feet on the other side of my head. Of course, if he could stick the landing, he would get 10's all around and smile from ear to ear and say, "That was just hooper!" Then, it would be Dex's turn.

Frayne would take a pass at this game.

But now the full-grown boys are packing two-bills-plus each, so I also take a pass at this game.

My kids think I'm alright.

But they think I'm forgetful, like the time I was preaching, and I said, "So, (A), the first thing is…and (B), the second thing is…and (3) the third thing is…and (4) the last thing is…" They all three came up to me at 10:15 and said, "A-B-3-4, Dad?" And then, of course, I did it again in the second service and heard, "A-B-3-4, Dad?" again at 12:15.

My three boys think I'm tough. I know they think this, because it is reflected in their wide-eyed stares upon the recognition of my manly feats of daring and verve. (That is a cool book title: Manly Feats of Daring and Verve, except I only have enough to put into one little chapter, so that one will have to wait.) Or maybe, their saucer-sized eyes are just reflecting how incredulous they are that I would do certain things to certain things.

Like when I popped the rattlesnake.

Yeah, seriously. I popped a rattlesnake.

This happened in northern California at a place that we call the Railroad Park Hotel, but I'm not sure that's its name. We liked to stop there pre-Kenny, because the Littler Fellers and Frayne and I could all fit in one caboose. (Luckily, none of us had too big of a caboose, if you know what I mean.) So there was this cool pool that we could swim in (if it wasn't

February, and our hair wasn't spiked purple), and a steel bar up in the caboose that the boys could hang and swing from. (One time, we took a picture of Kyle swinging from that bar, and then we got double prints and when we put the pictures in the photo album side-by-side, it looked as if we had twins, but that would confuse people, and they would say, "Where's that other boy?" and we would look sadly downcast at the floor and shake our heads and say, "Oh...that's Kevin, Kyle's twin brother. We sold him." And that seemed really funny at the time, especially when we said we got $2,000 for him, but now I think we should probably stop telling that story.)

There was also a plake at the RPH, and that is where I popped the rattlesnake. We were walking along, and all of a sudden, right there in our path next to the RPH plake slithered about a three-footer, rattling its way along. I bravely reminded the children and The Wife to stand back, while we let it slither on by.

When we went to leave the park, we all loaded up in the big gray 1986 Suburban, backed out of the parking lot and began to drive down the little frontage road next to the RPH. And wouldn't you know it, that ol' rattler just slithered out in front of us on that there frontage road! I, being vigilant and mindful with regard to camping safety, simply announced, "That rattler shouldn't be here in such a populated area! I am going to take care of THAT problem!" and squarely placed my front left tire about midpoint in that poor guy's body, gave a little gas and that's when the snake popped! It literally popped! I thought someone shot that rattler, but it actually just popped! I mean, really, really loudly popped! Then came, naturally, the squeals of both glee (boys) and disgust (wife) amid my harrumphing about how necessary that act of civil safety was!

After driving away and feeling just a touch guilty, I decided it wasn't good just to obliterate nature without taking some of the spoils, so I turned the Ballardmobile around and tracked that snake down to the gully into which its twitching-nerve-ending, loudly-popped body slid, and deftly cut off its rattle with my house key. What a mountain man!

My boys think I'm tough and maybe a little haphazard and risky and foolish at times.

The foolish factor came into play just a few years later. In the Carlsons' pool we were in Davis on a 105 degree day. (We used to say, "Oh, isn't it so delightful?" when it dropped under 90.) Davis is a pretty okay town, if you like it hot and dry and flat and brown and hot. Did I mention hot? Frayne and the ladies were sitting in the porch shade while the rest of us guys did guy swimming pool things like dunking and chicken fights and 1 1/4 flips off of the diving board (red-bellies) and ate chips and dip and drank soda and played Marco Polo and Keeper of the Chest and Escape From Alcatraz. Someone had randomly stuck a small inflatable donut life ring kind of thing on the end of the diving board. We had just finished a rousing game of See Who Can Hold His Breath Underwater the Longest (and had just sent the paramedics and ambulances away) when I said, and I admit this wasn't the most brilliant thing to come up with, "Hey Dex, I betcha ya' can't throw this little ball through that life ring over there."

The word 'betcha' contains in it the connotation that there is going to be some kind of remuneration-financial gain-reward to the one Little

Feller who can throw the little ball through that life ring over there. So, then came the inevitable question, "What'll you give me?"

Here is where I went completely wrong.

I had just done a music gig somewhere and gotten paid in cash—something I didn't get to see very often. So I took the five 100's and put them up on the top shelf of the cabinet above the bar where we ate our breakfast. Those 100's were brand new. Those 100's were crisp. Those 100's were my undoing. Knowing that I had them stashed away nice and safe up there, and they were essentially 'free money,' made me cavalierly, smugly, stupidly respond, "A hunnerd bucks." Then, figuring it was my out, I added, "But you have to do it with your eyes closed."

Without hesitation, LF #1 made his way to the center of the pool in the middle of the shallow end, turned his body sideways like a big league pitcher, stuck his left arm straight out in front of him (as a scope), shut his eyes and let fly.

I'm not exaggerating when I report this.

The ball cleanly, and I mean *cleanly*, cleared the inside of that impossible target, straight through the daggoned middle of the itsy bitsy teeny weeny yellow polka dot life ring! So the stupid old bald man with hair on his back stood there aghast and jaw-dropped while what seemed like every overly-thrilled woman and child in the flat, hot, brown, dry land of Davis, California screamed for hilarity and great joy!

Then the next inevitability from LF #2, "Well it's only fair if I get to try!"

Without hesitation, LF #2, (you'll notice some similarities to the content of the earlier paragraph) made his way to the center of the pool in the middle of the shallow end, turned his body sideways like a big league pitcher, stuck his left arm straight out in front of him (as a scope), shut his eyes and let fly.

I'm not exaggerating when I report this.

The ball again went through that dinky little opening in that stupid little life ring!

Women and children everywhere hollered, while I went submerged to get away from it all.

When I surfaced, there was great jocularity and high five's, and in every word and action rang these true words: "Boy, Dad sure is stupid."

LF #3 then lined up, and bless his little heart, he was just a little twerp at the time and couldn't quite make it the length of the pool, so I was able to offload, transfer, whatever you call it, all of the finger pointing by calling him a little loser. I'm so glad he was there and missed. (Just kidding.)

Then, I said, "Double or nothing" to the big boys.

They passed, officially, but, and this is just stunning to me, Dex actually did it again!

I think I owe Kyle about $94,100 right now. $100 is for a dumb little bet I just made (you'd think I've learned) about something I thought his mom would say and she didn't—and then $94,000 for shooting a wadded up paper towel all the way across the room into my thin-mouthed water glass. (I told him I would match what the girl on *Deal or No Deal* just got offered, and he actually thought I meant it, and he made the shot, and what a crazy kid to actually think I actually meant it. I mean, come on.... $94,000?)

The boys think I'm tough, haphazard, a little foolish and somewhat clumsy. I sometimes forget to watch where I'm going, and I sometimes walk into things like pillars and columns and canyons and moving trains and stuff like that. They think this is pretty funny, but not as much as Frayne does, especially if I draw blood. They all laugh at different things, like the time we were having a Nerf war, which included everything that can be shot or thrown safely within a house, like Kush balls and darts and little arrows and kettles and televisions and bricks. Kyle once stuck his little head up behind the couch and I, seeing my great opportunity to knock his block off, threw something (that I don't remember being that hard) and it missed his head wide left and high and shattered the glass of one of our original art pieces. (When I write it that way, it sounds as if we have a home gallery or something, but it's really not like that.) Glass showered down on poor Kyle, and the couch and the floor, and we all just laughed and laughed rolling-on-the-floor-laughter, and I just picked up all the little pieces and figured Frayne would never know the difference. We boys thought we were pretty smart putting that all back together! Took her maybe .00035 seconds to notice when she walked through the front door. She didn't laugh as hard as we boys did, which is really kind of sad for her, because, boy, we sure had a lot of fun.

Another time, I was busy talking and cooking (mac and cheese) and I turned to put the saucepan on the stove and the milk in the refrigerator, but I was talking, remember, and so I put the full, plastic one gallon milk jug on the stove and the saucepan in the refrigerator and turned to get the saucepan on the stove, but remember I said it was in the refrigerator, so that's where things started to go south, because I then picked up what I thought was going to be the saucepan, but was actually the full, plastic one gallon milk jug, remember I said it was on the stove, and in so picking it up poured milk all over the stovetop and counter out of the four or five holes which transformed the full, plastic one gallon milk jug into a beautiful spewing fountain of down pouring milk. I didn't put it then into the refrigerator, you'll be glad to know.

So intelligent, hard-working, charming, attractive, insightful…those are all the things I firmly and humbly believe I am, while my kids, I'm sure, would agree, though they would add a few more adjectives to the list. I can only hope that their descriptors (complete with eye-rolls and snickers) will include a few like 'unconditionally loving' or 'always there' or 'out for my best' or, at the very least 'funnier than heck.'

6
My Hobby is Mountaineering

I've never died on a mountain. I'm named Fortunate.

I thought you might get a kick out of hearing about some of my outdoors adventures. There's always something fun to tell about a mountain ascent, that is, unless you ruin something like a leg or an arm or a tent or a friendship.

Before I jump into this, however, let me just say that I am not an expert. I know two things about mountain climbing: 1) The mountain lets you climb it. 2) The mountain never makes it easy. Past that, all that's really required is some decent gear, a decent body, (I'm so fortunate to have kept my girlish figure all these years), a little decent common sense, and a decent amount of drive.

Now that I'm putting that list together, I realize how deficient I really am.

My gear is garage sale gear at best. I lost my right crampon (which in non-technical terms is that spiky little thing you slap onto the bottom of your boot so you can climb up glaciers and ice, but can also use to put holes in tents or climbing partners) on some descent somewhere (you don't have to have a good memory to be a mountain climber). So, you can picture a solid left step and then what?! My pack is an external frame (means the frame is on the outside) that looks pretty old. It really is old. Not cool. I have an ugly green and purple 80's vintage jacket that I've used for over twenty years, except now I have this big parka thing with fur around the hood that I took to Kazakhstan with me, and maybe I'll start using that.

This reminds me of the time I was standing in this Kazakh church, and this big Russian-looking guy came in and looked at me in my fur-lined coat and said, "Fat chicken." I was rather stunned and said, "What?" (Pretty intelligent, huh?) And he said, "Fat chicken." And I said, "Fat chicken?" (Equally intelligent.) And then I found out later that he was saying, complimentarily, "Fat jacket." Oh. Okay.

Now, the whole body thing. I feel like I'm twenty-five at times (usually when I'm in a prone position on the couch watching March Madness), and I feel like I'm seventy-five at times (usually when I'm upright and vertical.) Here's the list of things: I'm pre-diabetic. I have high cholesterol. My pinkies and thumbs have been basketball-jammed numerous times, and they hurt. My left shoulder feels a little stiff, and my right elbow is in occasional pain. On top of all that, the core of me is suspect, as I don't do the crunches that I should, and I had an L5-S1 discop…discogr…disclop…disc surgery about three years ago.

With regard to the common sense, it might be good to refer back to the whole 'betcha-can't-throw-this-little-ball-through-that-little-hole-with-yer-eyes-closed' story. In all actuality, I have a touch of summit fever, which can kill you, which is worse than getting cut from the Anacortes basketball team (I'm over it) or losing a hunnerd bucks. Summit fever is that malady that one gets when he can see, feel, taste the top of the peak and will not, cannot let himself not get there. Again, this has never killed me, per se, but it has done so in a few of those who indulged in this particular pastime.

I do have the drive to climb, once I've made the drive to wherever I'm going. If it's safe, I'm *going to get to the top.*

There have been little tits (molehills) climbed, like Table Rock (which looks like a, you guessed it, table) and some things in the Sierra and those day hikes you take when you're out camping or backpacking and you want to get on top of things. And those all have stories attached to them, like when Fisch (Fischback, last name) and I were going on up to Lake Mildred in Washington state, and those mice skittered across my sleeping tarp, back and forth next to my head all skittery night long in the moonlight, and then that one adventurous and totally inappropriate mouse snuck into my sleeping bag through the zippered hole down at my feet and skittered excitedly up the inside of my leg to my crotch…how quickly can a person get out of a mummy bag?! Or the time Kyle and I were hiking above Tahoe and had just made this little summit and turned a corner, and there was a real bear standing there, and it just looked at us and then lumbered on off down the trail without attacking us, which was kind of disappointing because saving my son from being mauled would have been an excellent story to tell, especially being armed only with a walking stick, except then I might have had to start this whole chapter with, "I once died on a mountain." (I got Kyle good about twenty minutes later when he was leading the way up the trail in quiet meditation, and I snuck up behind him and jumped him and roared, "Aaarrgh" like a bear would (I guess that's more like "Grrrrr") and he jumped himself about high enough to drive a Hummer under! Oh, that was funny!)

But, I want to talk about the big climbs. Those around or over 10,000 (hear me grunt and snort in a manly way) feet.

I could go in order of elevation, or chronologically. Hmmm. Or easiest to most epic. Let's see. Or it could be least favorite to most favorite. You're saying right now, "Just pick one."

Okay.

South Sister, Oregon, was my first conquest. If you have a nasty mind, you are thinking I'm referring to a girl during my high school days that lived over near Mt. Erie. That's not what I'm talking about. South Sister is the third in the chain of three, the other two being (I bet you can guess this, Middle Sister and North Sister. I hope you weren't thinking Not-So-South Sister and Really-Not-So-South Sister, because that would have been really random, and I'd be worrying a little about you.) Aside from the five of us guys skinny-dipping in Green Lake, I just remember chugging my little (re-clothed) behind up nearly vertical scree, with my old garage sale pack and boots and other obsolete gear, and these two high school students from the local cross country team jogging past us on up to the summit. Jogging! As in running slowly! As in faster than walking!

Mt. Shasta, not the tallest, but the largest mountain in the contiguous United States (I know that word, because Dex was in the geo bee at his school in fifth grade and got a question about the contiguous U.S. incorrect and was thusly, shamefully, booted from the stage, and that was hard for me to watch.) It's what we call in the industry a 'fourteener.' Shasta can be climbed a bunch of different ways, but the standard approach is from the south-southwest side, from about 8000'. After climbing over a bit of a ridge, you just hunker down at about 10,000' for the night.

I found out that some things can change overnight…like the weather and one's enthusiasm for climbing.

We set up tents like you're supposed to and then began to think about eating. I don't mind telling you that it was colder than an (we like to say this in our family, but it's totally inappropriate) ice blocking witch's butt in a Minnesota coal mine in February. (That's pretty dang cold, and if there is a witch out there named Gertrude, then I'm really in trouble.) I had borrowed a little hiking stove from my friend Scott, and we were trying to get it fired up. I should be more honest. This was a special, pristine, Swedish stove that Scott had had since his childhood, and it didn't have a mark on it.

We torched it.

Blackened it.

Fried it.

Toast.

But we got it going, which made boiling water a lot easier than if we hadn't. (Scott later forgave me for returning a block of charred metal.)

After our delectabilities and libation, (which were probably some kind of freeze-dried pork and beans and water), we slipped into our little red tent for the night, not without taking a quick look at the numerous stars and the lights of the city thousands of feet below. Just a stellar night altogether.

Then, the wind began to blow.

Somewhere along about 2 a.m., we sensed some fluttering of our tent walls. This is the understatement of the year. I don't even know how to describe it, except maybe to picture yourself in a convertible MG driving down the road at 140 and trying to keep your wits about you. Very, very, very windy.

Up went the stakes. Up went the tent. Up went everything not tied down, including gloves and, (Oh! Hey, maybe that's where my other crampon went!!!) I remember thinking at the time, "Someday, we're going to look back on this and laugh."

We did eventually summit on a calm and beautiful blue sky day…passed on the way by a ranger who had spent the night in a snow cave, one night of over one hundred that he had summited Shasta.

Mt. Adams is just over 12,000' and located in Southwest Washington. A good climb. Big ol' dome.

Then, there are four peaks within just a few miles of where we lived in Colorado. The Estes Cone is just over 10,000', the Twin Sisters are around 12-something, then St. Mary's and the muthah-uv-em-all, Longs Peak, the highest point in Rocky Mountain National Park.

I climbed the Sisters alone. The first attempt, which was with a group of friends, was thwarted (on an amazingly clear late night with a full moon so bright that we could see colors and shimmering snow and stars a-plenty and a thunderstorm raging over Ft. Collins, forty miles to the northwest) by one of our rookie climbers who got a little goofy because of the altitude. We knew he was goofy, because he was saying things like, "Wow, little purple bunnies have eaten up my tennis shoes." Once we figured out that he wasn't talking in mountain climber code, we just went on back down with him, which was really disappointing, because it could have been a really romantic evening—except that there was really no one there to be romantic with, because Frayne didn't really dig the climbing thing due to her pregnancy thing. (I always appreciated, however, that there was often good vittles like roast beef and mashed potatoes and gravy or waffles and such upon our return, which was a great perk of the pregnancy thing, not to mention Kenny when he arrived on the scene.)

So that leaves us with Longs Peak, and without going into a whole lot of detail, let me just say that I think I came up with one of my best lines ever, if I do say so myself, upon our long descent. Here's what happened.

Longs Peak usually requires an overnight stay at about 11,000', prior to the final 3,000' ascent. This happens at a place called the Boulder Field. (You can probably imagine what this looks like.) The next requirement is a traverse to and through a rock formation called the Keyhole. (You can probably imagine what this looks like.)

This leads to the back side of the mountain and a long, arduous route that sometimes isn't the easiest to find. But no worries! They (okay, now I have to just mention the whole 'they' thing, because isn't it weird how there is no 'they' and we just call them 'they' when 'they' really don't exist?), in this case probably meaning rangers of some sort, have put little round paintings here and there on rock faces and cliffs in order for climbers to easily find their way up the mountain. These 'targets' are easily spotted and placed at regular intervals.

I was climbing with my friend, Thomas, a very experienced rock climber, but not so much a mountaineer. He was leading, and I was trusting. I was paying attention mostly, except for when I wasn't, and it was about an hour and a half after seeing the last 'obvious' target, that I realized I wasn't seeing them any more. This was a bit of a cause for concern. Not wanting to be a back seat hiker, I waited and waited and waited to mention this until I just couldn't stand it any longer. "Uh, ahem, er, Thomas," I sputtered, "Could it be that we are off route?"

He didn't take long to agree, and I muttered something sarcastic and biting, which he utterly deserved.

So around we turned to find our way back to the 'obvious' targets that we had 'obviously' missed—a three-hour tour, three-hour tour.

Long story short, we made our way to the top, singing Steve Taylor's 'Finish Line' and making up funny and rummy, non-brain-functioning altitude-impacted lines like, "And I saw you fall on your can, and I saw you holding my hand, and I saw you crash down and land at the finish line," or "I saw you barfing your guts, and I saw you acting real nuts, and I saw you act like a putz at the finish line," which do not do any worthwhile justice to this wonderful, inspiring song, but you do what you've gotta do to make it to the top.

We took pictures and had one of Colorado's most glorious summits all to ourselves on the prettiest day of the year.

We down climbed and passed back through the elohyeK and dleiF redluoB and continued on down past alpine tundra, closer and closer to tree line. Suddenly, a snowball came whizzing fast and thunked me right smack dab in the back of the head! I whirled around and both complimented and complained with a "Nice shot!" Thomas' reply was simply mean-spirited and oh, so painful: "Not hard. Just had to aim for the big bald spot!"

That's when the greatest-one-liner in all of mountaineering history was uttered by Yours Truly:

"It's the only target you've hit all day!"

I share these mountaintop experiences for the sake of all who have ever spent time in the valley (of the shadow of death), and I recount these with great reverence and joy! Climb every one of them, enjoy the view on the way up, at the top, and on the way back down. That's what I try to do.

7
My Career is *Not* Security

I've been physically assaulted twice in my life, not counting my children surrounding the event of Flip-Around-Thingie. I don't really think you're a real man unless you've had someone uncork one on you. And you're not a real man's man unless you've popped some unsuspecting victim right in the chops—especially if he's small and defenseless and chicken. (Just kidding.)

Pop #1 came during my junior year of high school at the hands of Mark Foigo. He happened to like Kim, whom I was dating at the time.

Kim was a very sweet girl. I really liked her a lot. She was a petite brunette cheerleader and humble and pretty, and we used to walk home together in the cold, right down 8th Street. I think we had about eight awesome blocks together from the high school to where 8th T'd with L, and she turned left, and I turned right, and that's when I would arrive home and go down the stairs to my little basement bedroom with the red carpet and play England Dan and John Ford Coley on my turntable and think, "That was really nice."

I think Foigo also sat in his basement room with his 12-gauge and his nun-chucks and brass knuckles, and he and his minions would confer and assemble their plans of how they were going to 'get that little choir faggot Ballard and teach him a lesson'. I may be overstating things here a little bit, because when it all came down, it was just Foigo and his right hook that got me. But I'm getting ahead of myself.

I mean you've got to have this pictured, right? This guy was the strongest and biggest football player, (next to our D1-bound lineman who was deep and wide, deep and wide, like the old Sunday School song says), wondering how on earth a jazz-singing 140-pounder like me could have any kind of chance with one of the in-your-dreams girls on campus. You know, I am really enjoying right now all of the angst I must have caused him, especially when I think of the Burlington-Edison running back who ended my promising football career in one swift hit. So here's to you, all of you musicians and artists and chess players and little people who get walked on and thumped and put down and...

I'm back.

I knew Foigo was going to do something on the particular day that he did. I was leaving our 8th and L house and mentioned this to my dad, and he said, "Just get in the first punch." I wish he had explained that to me, unpacked it a little more, because I just didn't understand it. I had always thought that the one who threw the first punch would be the first one to get thrown out of school, to be blamed. His words made sense later in the day.

One other thing I should mention. Not only was I choir boy, but I was also in the chorus of the school play, which happened to be *Bye Bye Birdie*. (Don Macy was Conrad Birdie.) My most vivid memory of this play was the bar scene where one of our guys was going to be slick and conniving and put real booze in the booze bottles, and that was great until one of the female cast members found out and switched out the booze for vinegar at the last second. That was fun to watch! I also have a memory here of our production the following year of *The Wizard of Oz*, in which Ken Witter was the Scarecrow and I was the Tin Man, and the Lion's tail fell off during one scene and magically made its way off-stage, being tossed from flat to flat to flat. That was pretty funny. We put on some interesting shows there in Anacortes.

So I'm walking through the cafeteria on said day and had just received my plate of tater tots and some kind of mystery meat and yellow corn, when all of a sudden there was a commotion, and wouldn't you know it, I'm right in the middle of it! Ol' Foigo is mouthing off about something, and I'm just standing there wondering if he's talking to me or about me, and it was surreal. I was holding my tray out in front of me with both hands, and literally all I remember is corn flying through the air. He caught me with that right hook on my left eye, and from there it was just a donnybrook. I have no idea what a donnybrook is.

I had duked it out with my bro out in the driveway—even had some boxing gloves. But this was different. And it was different than the movies too! It was not scripted. It was not choreographed. It was not well-timed. It was just mental, physical, emotional, pandemonium and crazy free-for-all fracas flailing. I'm not sure what a fracas is. I really don't remember the fight, except that I think at one point it went from punching to grappling to holding-on-wrestling, and I do remember clearly that it took six guys to pry us apart. It was quite a broo-ha-ha.

That evening, I had to put on makeup to cover up my big black eye, so take that Foigo, not only was sweet Kim being dated by a 'choir faggot,' but she was hanging out with a 'choir faggot in mascara!'

Things with Kim didn't work out so well in the long run. Can't remember who she dumped me for—probably someone who didn't wear mascara. I don't know what mascara is, actually. Not sure if that's the right word for what I was wearing. But dump me she did, (swell violins), just like every other pre-Frayne girl I ever had an interest in.

Pop #2 came later. After living in the dinky little puny house in East Multnomah County, we moved to another church-owned dinky little house in Portland. Part of the agreement of this new church and the accompanying housing, was that I would provide 'security' for the church, which was right across 45th from our new place. A pretty sweet gig except for the second assault on my life which occurred while I was 'making my rounds.'

A quick little mention here about our very first dog, pre-kids. Her name was Xantha—The Golden One. There are so many funny stories about Xantha. She was also pre-Kelly, and when she was owned only by Frayne, she once brought home a shrink-wrapped-in-store-plastic package of hamburger! Another time, we were sunbathing on a dock on the Willnobyl, and that little Welsh Corgie-Lab mix thought someone was calling her, because Olivia Newton John was somewhere in that boom box singing, "Xanadu. Xanadu-u-u." She once escaped from our Portland yard and got on a Tri-Met bus, and she must have been really surprised when Frayne's friend who happened to be on that very bus recognized her and said, "Xantha, no! Go home!" But the best was when she got a ticket for being a 'traffic hazard', and my brother had to go to court to bail her out!

Xantha is also out at the farm, in her own eternal space out there in the orchard.

But she was with me the night of the big bang.

We were walking across the parking lot, kitty corner (katty corner to some) from our house. I smelled him before I saw him, because he was smoking a cigar. Out from behind the brick out building just to the west of the back entrance, he emerged. He walked right toward me, a big stocky guy. I should have saw it a-comin'. He just walked right up to me without slowing down, pulled his arm back and let fly, catching me right behind my left ear.

I am proud to say that I did not go down.

I am proud to say that I did not cry like a little girl.

I am proud to say that I stood my ground and took it like a man.

I am proud to say that when he said, "Don't f--- with me." I was tough enough to say right back to him, "I'm not f-----g with you." That was pretty hardcore of me, I think.

Needless to say, I took little Xantha right home and scolded her for not ripping the guy's face off.

After that, I called the cops, that is, once I could stop shaking long enough to dial the phone.

This lady police officer came and took down the information that I had for her.

I went and acquired some pepper spray and a baseball bat.

And then, I waited.

About a week and a half later, I was driving out of my driveway, and *there he was again*. Only this time, he was lurking in the bushes, peering into the windows of our pretty neighbor. That didn't seem right to me. Time to act, Ballard! So, fumbling with terrific and extremely shaky nervousness, I quickly ran into the house and, once I could stop quaking long enough to dial the phone, called the authorities again.

They were there lickety-split.

Guns drawn, they cornered the guy and cuffed him and led him back to their cars.

That's when I got *really* tough! I walked right up to that cigar-smoking, fist-throwing, window-gawking, bad man, and I shook a finger in his face and reminded him of how he wasn't welcome here. How shameful is that?

My awareness of these types is becoming more and more acute. I remember a guy at The Space Needle McDonald's coming back to pick a fight with me and how smart I was to actually set my Big Mac and fries and Diet Coke down on top of the trash cabinet thing, which made him run for fear, because he knew I was ready for him. So, I just keep getting scarier and scarier.

But the thing I'm learning more than anything else, is when someone wants to engage me in an angry moment, it's best to probably just follow the advice that we've all heard all our lives and turn the other cheek. I get flipped off sometimes when I'm driving, (really not sure why, given I'm only cutting in and out of traffic lanes at a high rate of speed), and I always respond with the V signal peace sign. It's amazing how disarming that is to those slow pokes.

It's just not worth it sometimes.

Peace.

8
My Degree is Terminal

I went to nine colleges.

I started out at Western Washington University, ran out of money and moved home and attended Skagit Valley College. From there I joined a music group at Green River Community College, which led me down the wrong road, if you know what I mean. So I moved to Phoenix, Arizona to attend school for home design, which lasted about three weeks. Trinity Western University took me the following year and I (Yahoo! Hurrah!) actually finished my two year AA degree. Then I got into the church and took a course at North Park College in Chicago and enrolled full-time at Warner Pacific College, where I got both my BA and Masters. I 'finished' up at George Fox University, which granted me a doctorate in leadership.

Whew!

Wait. I'm missing one.

WWU...SVC...GRCC...PIT...TWU...Oh yeah...Mt. Hood Community College. Nine. 9. Nice number.

Why am I telling you this? Certainly it's not to brag! I always looked up to the people who just left high school and matriculated forthrightly and went four years to one state school and then stayed on and got their graduate degrees and took jobs and did everything right. That seems to be much simpler than my silly path.

I think I just bring it up because all the little steps along the way have had some pretty good moments associated with them!

Like Trinity, for example. I was such an immature college student there! All I cared about was (a) being noticed, and (b) being noticed. If my sense of humor was at all present in high school, it was only magnified once I was out on my own, free to act however I chose. Oh man. Freedom and my sense of humor. Not good.

So a couple of us took to that whole shenanigan thing again. We really liked to go into the dorms at three in the morning and shut off all the breaker switches. Then we would go through all of the open rooms, tip-toeing around sleeping brothers and sisters (I'm fiendishly smiling right now) and turn on everything electronic that we could find: stereos, TV's, radios, lights, hair dryers, toothbrushes, anything that had noise associated with it! Then we would sneakily tip-toe back down to the breaker box and throw the switch and then laugh and laugh and laugh over how innovative and unique and clever we were!

But my most favoritest of all (I'm hunched over the computer, fiendishly smiling AND rubbing my hands together now) was the ol' key-clanking-against-the-window trick.

There was one Christian sister that we didn't like very much. (I know now that this is not the way Jesus intended for us to live, so you don't have to get in touch with me to set me straight.) So we snuck a girl into her room with a tack, fishing line, and a house key. She tied the key to the fishing line, about eighteen inches from the end, then reached out the icky girl's window and tacked that line into the outside wall just above her window, then dropped the rest of the fishing line down to the ground. She sneakily tip-toed back outside her room and we waited for night to fall. (Isn't this getting exciting?! Wa ha ha.)

We then ran the fishing line across the quad and hunkered down behind a bunker. (Hey—that's a Hinky Dinky! Bunker hunker. Here's how you play: You come up with a word for 'bunker,' like 'trench' and then you come up with a word for 'hunker,' like the word 'crouch,' and then you say 'trench crouch' and the person who is listening has to come up with what you mean by saying two rhyming words, hence 'bunker hunker.' A Hink Dink is one syllable. A Hinkity Dinkity is three and a Hinkadilly Dinkadilly is four. The other day Frayne and I were walking and the CLUE words we came up with were a Hink Dink—wet pet—and the answer was a Hinky Dinky—soggy doggy—which we thought was extra bonus because the clue words don't have to be any kind of Hink anything. That was sweet!)

So hunker in that bunker we did in the middle of the night after everyone was asleep. When we pulled on that little string, of course, the key would be raised up above the level of the top of the window—out of sight. But putting slack in that little string would render that little key susceptible to gravity and it would clink clink clink against that poor Christian sister's dorm window.

Schwoop would go the curtains!

We would wait.

Back to bed she would go, then...clink, clink, clink.

Schwoop would go the curtains! On would go the light! We could see 'what the heck' written all over her face, which made us snicker and chuckle and 'sh sh sh' each other until the light would go off and we would wait and then…clink, clink, clink. (Timing is everything!)

Over and over and over again (when will she learn?!) and our snickers and chuckles made way to laughing and poking and hugging and true Christian community!

Many HD's come to mind: Dream scheme. Hot plot. Slick trick. Night fright. Vile smile. Joke poke. Happy clappy.

I remember when at Mt. Hood Professor Hal Malcolm stopped music theory right in the middle of class, split the room in two with his pointing finger, walked right up into my face and said, "You, son, have 'It.'" Highlight reel of my life right there. Ding ding ding. Nothing nicer could be said. And he followed it up with, "And listen to me because the last person I told that to ended up being the lead singer of Quarterflash."

Too bad I don't look good in Spandex!

Warner Pacific was just a lot of hard work since I was working in a church almost full-time and had two kids to care for throughout.

George Fox was sort of the same way.

The three weeks I spent in Chicago at North Park were the longest millennium I've ever lived through, but not as long as it was for Frayne, who picked me up at the airport upon my return—two chicken poxed children in tow. (It was also pretty strange to actually UPS my entire desktop computer and printer back there—long before the days of affordable laptops.)

Well, there are some thoughts about my circuitous collegiate journey. Fortunately, now I get to do some of the teaching rather than the studying, but I am always learning. I wouldn't have it any other way.

9
My Wife is One-Of-A-Kind

I just want to say this one thing about Frayne, for the record: Everyone likes her. She has no enemies, which is probably the highest compliment that I can think of, especially when I consider all the people I've hacked off in my life. I really know no one else like this—or like her.

Our life together is filled with some very good memories—mostly of times when she showed why everyone likes her.

First, she has a caring heart.

For the first eight months of our time up there on that mountain property in Colorado (remember, when I was out gallivanting around on mountain peaks and such?) Frayne had to endure all kinds of physical and mental and emotional and relational transitions. We moved there in February (from sunny California, no less) when the wind was blowing snow sideways. And we lived at altitude, which is not easy on anyone. On top of all that, we moved into a little cabin off of Highway 7 that was not ready for our arrival. Okay, that's really an understatement. Not ready, as in no kitchen sink or cabinets, no dishwasher, no shower. No carpet and no linoleum. It was a stinky, depressing not-quite-completed remodel. (I had thought my friend, Brian, and I had done a good job of driving the U-Haul twenty-five hours through Nevada, Utah, and Wyoming—though the centrifugal force of my Rawlins, Wyoming taking-that-curve-too-fast moment almost put Brian's sleeping head in my lap and us in some rancher's cow pasture—unpacking all of our stuff, cleaning the cabin, setting up furniture, and so on. But I've come to learn that guy standards and gal standards are sometimes not equal on things like whether or not the kitchen smells greasy.)

Adding it up: Cross-country move with two little kids, altitude sickness, stinky and unfinished house, new job, cold and blowing snow.

Oh yeah.

Frayne was like ten weeks pregnant at the time.

In between throwing up because of the altitude and throwing up because of the smell of the kitchen and throwing up because of her pregnancy, Frayne was taking the boys out in the snow to walk over to the public restrooms for showers and the brushing of teeth.

Maybe that wasn't a very fun time for us.

I'm sure it wasn't a very fun time to be around me.

But, she adjusted, and the time came for Kenny's birth. Here is where the caring heart part really kicks in. Her pre-popping signs all came at like 3:00 in the morning (like contractions and water breakage and girlie stuff like that), so we loaded up our little Honda with all of the baby-having accoutrement, and began our drive to the hospital in Estes Park, ten winding miles to the north and 2000 feet down in elevation. Round and round and round we went past all of the trees and rocks and black-as-night Colorado mountain features. Rounding one of the final turns, we were greeted by a most curious sight. A huge bull elk stepped out onto the highway in front of us. But, something seemed amiss. I flashed my brights, and we could clearly see that this elk had something wrong with it, for there was something foreign in its antlers. We inched closer and closer, until we could obviously make out that this poor guy had wrapped himself up in somebody's mini-blinds!

"Oh, we have to help him," my absolutely-about-ready-to-give-birth-to-our-third-child wife said.

Hmm. I'm still trying to picture her out there waddling around saying, "Whoa there big fella, easy now, let me just reach up here and untangle those for you. Now, now…that's right. And remember…you can avoid this next time if you'll stay out of people's flowerbeds and quit sticking your head through their windows."

Frayne also knows how to make the best of a tough situation.

Another not-so-great time in our married life together was the time we spent 'on the road'. I had figured eight months of doing concerts and seeing every state east of Kansas would be inspiring and life-giving and fun and 'my big break'. I figured she figured the same, but then again, I was only like twenty-three at the time and twenty-three male stupid is a lot less informed than my current forty-seven male stupid.

So, we put everything in storage, flew across the country, and hooked up with this group called The Spurrlows. Such a great name. It was the fusion of the founder's first name (Thurrlow) and his last name (Spurr), which reminds me of a pastor I had once in high school who we laughed at because his name was Thurlow Yaxley, and then we really laughed when we found out his middle name was Dudley. Thurlow Dudley Yaxley! But, he was a good guy, and we respected him once we got used to his silly, sing-songy name.

Out on the road, we sang and played and took offerings every night of the week and two or three times on Sunday mornings. We would roll into town, eat whatever was offered us (often spaghetti or lasagna, and when we were in Louisiana, we had gumbo five nights in a row, and I remember the lady in Toronto asking us at dinner, "Now what do you absolutely hate to eat for lunch, since I'm providing your sack lunches tomorrow?" and I said, "Ugh, no more ham and cheese…just can't take that!" while Frayne—who had a view to the kitchen—was kicking me under the table repeatedly, because I was twenty-three-year-old-stupid, and sure enough, we opened up those sack lunches while we were riding Big Blue, and you guessed it…), set up for the evening concert, tear down afterward, sit on the stage and wait for our host homes, drive home with them (either to 'missionary' or 'mansion' experiences), stay up until all hours of the night explaining how we got to be so famous, sleep in all kinds of beds (one time, it was six out of seven nights in bunk beds), eat grits for breakfast in the South and whatever the rest of the country served us the rest of the time, ride back to the church (sometimes this was a huge adventure), get on the bus, and drive anywhere from two to twenty-four hours to the next venue. One time, we made a fifteen-hour trip in about thirty hours, because Bob and Beau put the equipment trailer into a cornfield in Iowa. That was pretty lame.

At the next venue, we would do it all again. About 200 times we did this.

Since Frayne didn't have any performance responsibilities on this tour, she was able to get creative with her fun. She used to really like to run the spotlight, because while the audience was focused on the guy who was doing the talking, she could focus focus focus that bright light right down into my face smaller and smaller and smaller until I beamed like a little angel. She thought that was hilarious. One night, she snuck backstage and went along the back of the highest riser while all us guys were standing up there and schwooped all of our socks down our shins (very uncomfortable), while we stood there with our game faces on, unable to do anything about it! Another time, she thought it would be funny to do the old sew-their-pants-legs-together-in-the-dressing-room trick, which I completely appreciated, because I got to watch as all the guys stuck their legs in their pants and sat their looking quizzically, wondering what on earth was going wrong!

Something else that hits me about Frayne's playful side: She's very clever. We used to play a game every time we would come closer to a new town or city. The driver of Big Blue would boisterously announce, "Okay, it's tam for a contest." (That's not a spelling error. He had a great Southern accent, and he really sounded like that.) So whenevuh that tam kime, (whenever that time came), we would all get ready, because we knew that it was tam to guess the next great site that we were going to see. Frayne always guessed correctly, and she always guessed it first.

In Nawlins, it was the twenty-nine mile bridge over Lake Pontchartrain.

In Tampa, it was the Sunshine Skyway Sky Bridge.

Frayne guessed that we were going to go into a tunnel under the Chesapeake Bay.

And, I kid you not, she guessed The Boll Weevil National Monument in Birmingham, Alabama. Now that's impressive!

She's also got a no-nonsense side.

She broke up a fight ring in a church parking lot once, all a-little-over-five-feet of her.

She knows how to ride a horse and how to get one to behave.

She works at the high school as a detention-attendance lady. She is well-liked there and respected.

She warns me when I'm going to walk into something dangerous (literally and otherwise), reminds me of who might be trustworthy and who might not be, and will go to the mat for the safety and wellbeing of her children.

This is the girl I married twenty-five years ago and am still with today, and I guess what this means to me, is that there is really no such thing as twenty-one-year-old stupid or forty-seven-year-old stupid, or maybe, since she's a year younger than I am and she's still with me to this day, that there's such a thing as twenty-year-old and forty-six-year old grace.

10
My Dad is Everywhere

Most everything I've written so far has its kind of fun and playful side, and that's cool. I like that kind of writing and reading. I guess I need to run by you a few things that aren't so fun and playful, but they're also a part of life, right?

It's the whole dad thing. Brace yourself.

Let me begin by saying this: My dad is the most incredible person I have ever met. He is intelligent. He is strong. He is funny. My dad is hard-working. He has a heart of gold. He means well. He is aesthetic. He is mathematical. My dad is old-fashioned. He cares for certain people.

My dad used to joke about being a godlike pilot. He flew the 747 when it first came out in the early '70's. He continually upgraded. I remember the CL-44 and the 707, which were child's play compared to the 747. He was a copilot. Then, he was a captain. Then, he jumped from domestic flights to international flights, and I heard stories brought home not just from Anchorage and Seattle and Newark, but from Tokyo and Bangkok and Hong Kong. He also brought home accompanying ivory sculptures and paintings and kimonos for Mom, and he showed us how to make sukiyaki and taught us how to say 'gomenasai,' and I'm not sure what that means—maybe 'how are you?'

My dad is a big-statured, big-mouthed man. Tall. Built. Loud. Dominating. And, he's right about everything whether he's right or not. He just comes across that way.

I grew up believing everything my dad ever said to me or about me.

My dad was everywhere. There was no getting away from him.

Let me tell you about my sister, because this information will fit into my story.

Mary was the perfect girl. She was a 4.0 student. She was the homecoming queen. She played sax in the band. She dated the same guy for over two years. (I dated about six girls for about two months each, and they all dumped me for other guys, which probably has messed me up, but hopefully I'm over it.) Mary was a tall, pretty blonde. On top of all this, she was a three-year varsity starter in basketball and won the state tournament her junior year—an amazing athlete that went on to pursue college basketball and the Olympics.)

Because Mary was such a talent, and because the program at my high school in Anacortes was not up to my dad's standards, he chose to move us from 8th and L Streets to Bradshaw Road in neighboring Mount Vernon. That was a good move for Mary, and I was able to stay in Anacortes for my senior year.

Here's the beautiful part about this arrangement. Because my brother had graduated and my sister did not go to school where I went to school and because I had my own car(s), I could come and go to Anacortes as I pleased with no supervision and little accountability, I was a free man! (Except I wasn't a man yet, but it doesn't sound as colloquially correct to say, 'I was a free boy!' because that sounds weird, like I was shut up in some kind of basement or something.)

Oh, about my car(s)...

I always loved cars.

When I was in junior high school, I remember getting—or buying maybe—a little clock radio that was in the shape of a Duesenberg. (My most vivid memory of this Duesenberg clock radio is when I was humming 'Tie a Yellow Ribbon 'Round the Old Oak Tree,' which is kind of shameful, I guess, and I walked into my room and over to my headboard where the Duesenberg clock radio was sitting and just flicked on its little switch, and you know what song was playing on the radio right at that moment? 'Tie a Yellow Ribbon 'Round the Old Oak Tree'!!!)

In order, my cars were a 1926 Dodge touring sedan (basket case with wood wheels), an orange 1953 Mercury Monterrey, and then an eerily similar 1953 Ford Victoria (anniversary edition with the flathead V8 and only 63,000 original miles—the car that had the multi-toned horn that, when I sang along on a Middle C, would play a Db major seventh chord, which I don't think you find a lot of high school guys doing maybe), a 1962 Corvair Spyder convertible (red with a white top and a turbo-charged engine—a car that I myself fixed up and took my girl for a ride in, so proud was I, and she said, "Kinda noisy, isn't it?" and then dumped me for the Anacortes basketball player with the Italian name), a 1968 Toyota sedan (Crown something? Can't remember…), a 1968 Dodge Polara (that Grandpa Kenny gave me, which was really awesome, though one time, I was driving across the bridge from Oregon to Washington, on my way home from selling pianos at the mall in my three-piece suit, and a guy pulled up next to me, looked at the not-so-fancy, stock-white Polara and said, "What's the suit for?" which kind of irked me), a 1976 Datsun B210 (HoneyBee), that old 1965 Chevy pickup, a 1978 Toyota pickup (yellow, with canopy, that

Frayne and I used to take up to Crown Point and eat Chinese food and kiss-and-what-not and watch lightning storms in), a 1981 Honda Accord (best car I ever owned), a Taurus wagon, a Suburban, a Sable wagon, a Plymouth minivan (that we drove for three months on Oahu, called 'The Beach Mobile'), an Olds 98 sedan ('The Ghost'), a Contour sedan, a Toyota Sienna minivan, a 1991 Honda Civic (which my son has now), a 1996 Jeep Grand Cherokee (to pull Redemption, my new boat that I forgot to tell you about) and my current car, a 1997 Toyota Camry that I saved up and paid cash for, which is just great.

Pretty sexy list, huh?!

That's twenty cars of my own.

Plus, my dad's three that I drove and which provided some pretty vivid memories—two wrecks and one that should have been. I'll start with that one.

The 1976 Honda was taken by me and Ken Witter one day after school. Now, remember that I was a free man, and fifteen miles between me and the farm on Bradshaw meant Anacortes was mine! So, the *one and only time* I ever skipped school, I was driving up Commercial (dragging the gut, we called it) and last-second, split-second, in-the-twinkling-of-a-nano-second jerked that little Honda left, across two lanes of traffic into the Radio Shack parking lot, somewhere between 10th and 15th Streets, squealing 12" tires and all!

You're not going to believe this. Guess where Dad happened to be standing. Yeah, right there ON THAT VERY STREET CORNER AT THAT

VERY TIME. Ken simply dropped his jaw and said, "You're busted." And, boy howdy, was I.

My dad is everywhere, along with his accompanying look of disgust.

Wherein I was not allowed to drive the Glastrons on lakes where there was usually no danger, I was allowed to drive the new expensive cars on real roads with pavement and other cars and real people and drivers like me. Go figure. This allowance to drive was the case with Dad's brand new 1979 Peugeot 504. Nice car back then. Nice car. Nice car until I got behind the wheel anyway.

On the way home from the senior prom, my next new girlfriend and I decided to go watch the submarine races out at Skyline. (There weren't really submarines out there if you know what I mean.) Somewhere between the high school and the submarine docks (wink wink nudge nudge) I was paying little attention to my driving (wink wink nudge nudge) and remember hearing her scream, "Kelly!" and then a blurring cacophony of crashing steel and breaking glass and a heart that started pounding its way out of my chest. I'll cut to the chase here. She was fine…just a few bumps and bruises and a quick ride to the hospital, and she was cool, though not entirely happy with me at that point.

I had blown through an unmarked intersection at 8th and K and T-boned a wood-sided station wagon. Of course, I knew what to do: write down the dude's info, right? But no pen or pencil or Crayola had I, so I began knocking on neighborhood doors in that quaint little part of town. No one seemed to be home! Finally, a nice lady opened her door and brought me a little bucket of writing utensils. I grabbed one at random, went back to the scene, wrote down the info required and put the pencil back into my polyester Angel's Flight blazer.

I had already called Dad.

He then showed up.

He said the f-word.

He got me out of the ticket. (I had the right of way.)

My dad is everywhere.

That pencil I put in my pocket? Some months later, I happened to be wearing that same jacket, reached inside, pulled out that pencil and looked at the writing on the side of it: "Accidents are Avoidable." That was jaw-droppingly weird.

The next year, somewhere between Phoenix and Trinity Western University, I ended up driving my dad's 1979 Honda Civic over to Spokane. (Clearly, I was not on the shortest path from Point A to Point B, not unlike my entire life's trajectory at the time.) To make a really long story short, (oh, but I have to tell this one about why I was in Spokane in the first place, because my old high school 'streaking' buddy Ken wanted me to come 'party' with him, which we kind of did a little—two martinis and a beer, and that was about it for this lightweight—and how we also went to an IHOP for pancakes at 3 AM, and when we were leaving, we ordered two hot chocolates to go, and the buxom waitress brought them out and held them about chest high, and Ken remarked with enthusiasm, "Look at the size of those!" which made me guffaw and then bust out laughing because of my juvenile and inappropriate sense of humor!), it's important to know that

I was not in my best driving state of mind 'the morning after' if you know what I mean.

So, I went to change a cassette tape in my tape deck, and I looked down and veered off of I-90 and looked up in time just to see myself miss a little pole, and I re-veered and over-corrected and went zip zip zowie fishtailing down the interstate and ended up rolling backwards in the farmland ditch, remembering, "This feels awkward." My wheels caught, and my (dad's) little Civic flipped over on its top. (The first flat-top Civic of its kind!)

I hung upside down for a minute picturing an explosion and my charred remains, then unbuckled, dropped, exited, and sat looking forlorn and perplexed out there all alone in The Palouse.

Then, this guy drives up in a little red 1979 Honda Civic, pulls over, gets out, walks up to my car and says, "Wow! I always wanted to see what the bottom of my car looks like!"

We rocked and rocked and rolled the car back over, and I got in and started it up.

And then, the fear hit me: "How am I going to explain this to Dad?"

So there was Dad, right out there in that early morning Ritzville ditch. I ended up driving the 220 miles home, my head sticking out the window all the way over cold Snoqualmie Pass, right on up to Dad's driveway, fear in my soul and the deepest desire to be anywhere in the universe but at 1513 Bradshaw Road.

Just the other day, my son Dex called and said, "Dad...everyone's okay...but..." His fault—a following distance kind of thing.

My response was simply, "Well, these things happen."

As you can tell in my writing, my dad was, is and probably will be everywhere, whether on Commercial and 17th or in the recesses of my constantly returning memory—reminding me of the wrong things and the right things to do and say at all the wrong and right times.

11
My Ideas are Unfolding

My Camry is gold. It has a driver's door. That driver's door has a pocket, and the pocket holds a notebook. It is a burgundy notebook. Said burgundy notebook is there for all of the ideas that I cannot contain upstairs. Therefore, I call it The Burgundy Brain.

The Burgundy Brain is there for my ideas, because ideas often come when I'm driving.

When ideas hit, I have no choice but to pull over to the side of the road and write them down. (This is because I try to keep my hands free for steering and talking on my phone and shaking my fist at the world and typing on my laptop and changing from my street shoes into my basketball shoes and drinking a latte and stuffing my turkey back into my sandwich and reaching down to pick up the chips that I dropped on the floor. I know that sounds a lot like multi-tasking, but at least I'm not as dangerous as those ladies in California who can change their babies out of dirty diapers or change out of themselves out of their sports bras while they're going 85 down Interstate 80 on the way home from the club.) So, you can see why it would be dangerous to write in my burgundy notebook while driving. The only problem with having to pull over, is that I (a) hate to be late, and (b) want to win The Game. Most guys know what The Game is. It has to do with (a) timing lights, (b) timing dangerous lane changes, (c) keeping an eye out for cops when doing anything more than 'five over,' (d) not letting anyone out-cut, out-maneuver, out-wit or out-get in front of you, (e) getting there two minutes faster than everyone else, (f) setting your own

DPR (driving personal record). These are all very important items for a guy. (I was pulled over the other day by a motorcycle cop who asked me if I knew how fast I was going 'back there', and I just said, "No idea," and he said, "Give me your license and registration," and I said, "I haven't had a ticket in at least ten years, and I really deserve one for all the times I haven't been pulled over," and he said, "Have a nice day," and boy, was I surprised…also a little disappointed, because he thwarted my attempt to make it from my house to the office in under :21.) I was playing The Game just the other day on the TSR (Tualatin-Sherwood Road), which is a great road for The Game, because it is always congested, and people drive 10-under as a habit. So, it was about 5:30 in the morning, and a stupid not-yet-awake guy was driving his big white panel delivery truck in the left lane, doing 35 in a 45. Inexcusable, guys. Come on. The problem for me, was that I, in the right lane, was coming up on a 10,000 gallon gas tanker truck in the right lane that was doing 32 in a 45.

Do the math.

In my attempt to both win The Game and avoid a catastrophic explosion and ensuing inferno, I whipped that little gold Camry Carrera of mine into that left lane with inches to spare between all of our collective bumpers. It was quite a move, fellow The Game players. Oh, do you feel me? (I looked around to make sure my dad wasn't standing on that particular street corner at that particular time, which, thankfully, he was not.) As you can imagine, Big White Panel Truck Delivery Guy was not pleased. Unfortunately, one of the rules of The Game is that you are required to stop for red lights. Red lights are like halftime, where everyone who *was* playing on the field now has to converge en masse in order to squeeze into the one little stadium tunnel that leads to their respective locker rooms. So, up pulls Big White Panel Truck Delivery Guy, and he's yelling and screaming and gesticulating, (I think that's what it was), through a long litany of profanities, to which I responded, "Uh…er…um…" As the light turned green, he blasted me with, "F--- you, you bald-headed faggot," which really hurt, because I'm not at all gay.

The Burgundy Brain contains song ideas.

And book ideas.

Relationship ideas.

Professional ideas.

The Burgundy Brain contains ideas that might just change the world. My friend, who is a film guy, made a movie that was pretty good. I liked it, and it made me cry. (Imagine, a competitive The Game player like me actually tearing up…) I was talking to him about it once, and he said, "I am hoping it makes it into the hands of all of the heads of state in the Middle East. I think if they could see it, then it could possibly end the conflict over there." Didn't sound arrogant or audacious at all. Just matter of fact. I like that, and it makes me cry if I think about it too much. I would like to be a part of an idea that changes the world.

My song ideas have to do with genre-busting innovation and groove and melody and lyrics and story. The hardest part about being a songwriter is really digging and respecting great artists and wanting to take something from their stuff and put it into my stuff while letting the emulating stop short of copying or plagiarizing. There really is nothing new under the sun, but every great artist really, deep down inside, wants to be the new thing under the sun that isn't. There are some pretty amazing genre-busting musicians out there—those who define musical paradigms that are truly unique and wonderful. In my dreams, I'd like to be one of them. That's a little tricky when you're a cross between Harry Connick Jr. and James Taylor and Sting and Take Six and Boston and Barry Manilow and Jars of Clay and that Canadian lady from the '70's that my friend Jeff loves so much…oh yeah, Ann Murray. (Just kidding about being like Ann Murray.)

I have a lot of song titles that are ready to go. By the way, that's how I operate. Quite often, something close to a title pops into my head, and then I work the ideas out with groove and melody and lyrics and story. No offense to Country Western music, but it seems to be the style that this process was meant for. For example, the title *Too Square to Get Around* came to me one day. Has a bit of a ring to it, right? It could be a song about marital fidelity—or a flat tire, for that matter. Here's one that just came to me as I was sitting here: *Stop Right There Before You Get Me Going*. That one is definitely about a woman—of either the seductress or nag type, depending on the mood of the songwriter:

> *Like a drippy faucet your demands keep coming down*
> *Baby, your persistence is the most irritating sound*
> *I try to keep my patience, but my agitation's growing*
> *So you'd better stop right there before you get me going.*

Probably won't win me a Grammy.

Or the other version:

Like a summer rainfall, your voice is one sweet sound
And, baby, how you touch me knocks my strong defenses down
I can't hold it back no more, my desire for you is growing
So you'd better stop right there before you get me going.

Potential there. Sex sells more than conflict.

I'll keep at it.

My book title ideas are pretty good, I think: *The Kelly Ballard Story* (my favorite), *My Life and Times by Kelly Ballard* (my second favorite), *The Story of My Life* (you get it), *Wasco and the Zombie Truck, I'm Not In Your Junk, How the Western Church Went South, Worship Whores, The Sound of Your Own Voice, Beauty in the Dirt.* Mostly cheery stuff, I think. Please don't steal any of those, not that you'd probably want to, because I think any one of them could be pretty big, and that's all that matters to me right now.

My relationship ideas have to do with intimacy, which kind of stops their perpetuation and fruition. In short, guys who play The Game don't spend a ton of time and energy on intimacy. My main Big Intimacy Idea has to do with what was called 'Jr. High' back when I was a kid. Or, we could just narrow it down to the Primary and Foundational Core Experience of Intimate Antithesis: Seventh Grade. I think, it is a universal truth that everyone has to go through some kind of experience that we can call Seventh Grade. I went to Seventh Grade in a fancy community where every other guy at my school—particularly, the 'jocks'—wore Hang Ten t-shirts (with the little gold feet embroidered on the front) and Puma sneakers (with the little logo on the side.) I wore neither. I also didn't have very much hair on my legs (like the gas station owner's son), which was cool, because I was also really scrawny. Wayne Carlton and Scott Nilson and Richard Werner had both hairy knees and muscles. On top of which, the girls that liked them, (Lori, Cami, Tina, for instance), all looked really nice in cheerleader skirts, and their breasts were full. Well, you know what you are when you have hairy knees and muscles and athleticism and nice clothes and full breasts: popular. Without those characteristics, I was, well, just as 680 out of 700 students at my junior high: regular. But, our collective Seventh Grade experience—wherein we want to move from 'regular' to 'popular'—taints us for life. I can still see people today operating in Seventh Grade mode, full of insecurity and self doubt and longing for better bodies, better things, and better notoriety. So, my Big Intimacy Idea is that we restructure our schools so that, just as an elevator may not have a 13th floor, we go right from Sixth Grade to Eighth Grade.

My professional ideas are also usually bad ideas, so I don't do much with them. Here's one: I think I could be President of the United States. (I haven't made it a goal...yet.) There is no reason that I couldn't start right now and make every minute of every day count toward being the President of the United States. I could go back to school. I could get my law degree. I could run for the School Board (and eliminate Seventh Grade.) I could pour myself into World History and Geography and finally know where places like Cote d'Avoire are. I could understand despots and world currencies and war strategies and power struggles and how to play The

(Political) Game. Again, if I were to be willing to (most likely) sacrifice my family and my friendships and my current good life, I could maybe-just-maybe, in twenty-plus years make a run for it.

I guess the reason I talk like that is make my other professional ideas seem not so bad. (Like the well known story about the young college student who wrote her parents:

Mom and Dad:

I love and miss you. By the way, I have dropped out of school because I'm doing a lot of partying. I fell and love and just moved in with my 35-year-old Physics professor.

Love,
Your Baby Girl

P.S. Please turn the paper over.

You know that on the other side was written: *'Oh, that was for perspective. I just need $100.')* So, to talk about wanting to have 100 acres up in the mountains where people who think about spiritual matters and write about them and want to lead and teach others to do the same doesn't sound so crazy, compared to the presidency. It doesn't seem so outlandish to want to partner with likeminded friends and colleagues in order to develop an open door space for artist-learner-leaders. It doesn't seem too much to think about horses and barns and performing arts centers and a faith community and recreation and mountain climbing and hiking and photography and concerts and silence and solitude and counseling and therapy of all types and the dissemination of gifted and equipped world changers who can transform organizations and businesses and institutions into venues of beauty and cooperation.

In lieu of a presidential bid, these types of ideas easily transfer over into the Ideas That Can Change the World category.

I can say this with confidence, because my craziest ideas are Jesus Ideas. Jesus Ideas are radical and revolutionary. My thoughts about Jesus can occasionally get me in trouble, because I like to explore Jesus in ways that the orthodox, dogmatic, Fundamentalist bent doesn't seem able to. The other day, I told some pastoral colleagues that even if Jesus were not the God-made-man that the Bible says he is, that I would dig his vibe anyway, because the values for which he stood and the modus operandi that he displayed are elements that I believe are the only answer to this global existential mess that we're in. (Unfortunately, these colleagues got out a really big wooden cross from the warehouse, lit a really hot fire underneath it, and then, when the coals were nice and toasty red, asked me whether I would prefer a right-side-up or upside down crucifix posture for my incineration. I said, "Oh, it doesn't matter," in an attempt to appear compliant. Good thing for me, because they didn't follow through.)

In my humble estimation, the revolutionary strength of Jesus resides primarily in the paradox he embodies—that power and position and posture thought of in ascendant terms are the very downward path. Conversely, it is the way of the self-sacrificial that really saves the day. It is only by the way of giving that we will ever receive the love (not popularity!) that we desire! It is through the emptying of the self, that a person finds his way to fullness—and not of the mammary type. (This is not *my* idea.)

As a matter fact, many of my selfish ideas just seem kind of lame when I look back at them. But maybe if I live simply and well and gratefully, the better ideas will come, and their accompanying dreams will be realized. Maybe that, in and of itself, is a pretty good idea.

12
My Mouth is Foot-Filled

I sometimes say dumb things.

I *often* say dumb things.

I try not to. I really do.

My friend Margot suggested to me a few years ago that I should consider 'self-editing.' I had never heard of that crazy concept before, but I think it just might have some merit.

Just the other day I was sitting with some men from the church, (actually, the elders of my church, to whom I am accountable) discussing my most recent oral presentation in front of our congregation. A pretty astute guy, (he's only a heart surgeon, not like he's a rocket scientist or anything), looked at me and gently asked, "Kelly, did you practice your talk?"

Long awkward pause.

I had, actually, practiced my talk, so I said, "Uh, yes."

And then, I risked a bit: "Why do you ask?"

"It seems it could have used a little bit of refinement."

There's something you should probably know about the church I'm in. For the most part, it's a lot like most other churches. People tend to want to spare people's feelings and certainly don't go looking for face-to-face confrontation. Combine those characteristics with a touch of grace and restraint on the part of our heart surgeon, (and a little bit of receptor insecurity), and it's easy to understand why the words, "It seems it could have used a little bit of refinement" translate into, "That was the suckiest talk I've ever heard by anybody, in any setting, anywhere."

But rather than fold, I considered the credibility of the source, the obvious validity of his question, and the importance of appearing non-anxious and non-defensive and replied kindly and wryly, "I see what you mean, but you know, my spontaneity is most of my charm."

I could have self-edited.

It's just, sometimes, I think I'm really clever or cute, and I just can't let the opportunity pass when I am on the verge of impressing or regaling the rest of the world with my winsomeness. It really is quite something and shouldn't just be wasted on my own self amusement.

You need to know, that even now as I write this, my cleverness has really caught up to me. I was just publicly humiliated by a guy who doesn't really dig my lingo…he feels I wield it as some sort of mockery and ridicule sword. I 'did the bad thing' in a church meeting just recently, and he let me have it. Of course, I figured everyone in the room would just tell him to be quiet and sit down, but there were nods and finger pointing and affirmation, and rotten tomatoes and slung mud and pea shooters and Bronx cheers (not sure what those are exactly) and even nooses being formed out of dinner napkins. That really made me pay attention.

Sometimes the ol' tongue just gets tied up.

Many months ago, my church undertook a major leadership change. The man who had been 'at the helm' for over twenty years was asked to take a different role, and I was 'promoted' to the position of visionary and head of the staff. We wanted to communicate this adjustment to our people in a timely and clear way, so we set aside one Sunday in August in order to tell the story and garner feedback. Needless to say, this was a bit of a tense moment, as people were trying to guess the 'story behind the story.' All went fairly well, however, with a good spirit in the room and apparent understanding on the parts of the listeners. Upon the completion of our explanation, I moved to the piano in order to lead a couple of songs, as well as participation in the Lord's Supper, Holy Communion. I don't know how it happened, but in the strangeness of the moment, when trying to invite the servers to bring the bread and the cup forward, I blurted, "Now it's time for the ushers to distribute the communion elephants."

And then I started ever-so-slightly grinning.

And the grinning gave way to snickering, which brought on chuckling, giggling, and then downright laughing!

The following week, I was inundated with elephant nick-knacks, statues, pictures, Internet stories, drawings, and other myriad pachydermal items.

Perhaps I should restore some of your trust in me by saying that we can and do sometimes say the right thing at the right time! (Let's deflect some credit here, and maybe acknowledge that Someone Else comes through in a Big Way when we've run out of anything good.)

I truly do love spending time with my boys. On Kyle's 11th Father's Day, we chose to go for a bike ride. (Oh, I should probably set this story up by letting you know that just two months prior, the Ballard family had purchased its first ever brand new car. Quite over-extended we were, getting into this first ever brand new car. We actually traded in two or three or four old-as-can-be-cars—each with 150-200K miles on them. So, this first ever brand new car was perfect, with the first ever brand new car smell and everything.) So, Kyle and I had quite a day together, pedaling down Songbird and over to Fellows and across Highway 99 to the local college, where we pedaled through the campus, paused under the giant oak, and shared blue Slurpees at 7-11. We talked. We laughed. We sipped. We pedaled home. Back we rode across 99, up Fellows, onto Songbird, and closer and closer to our house, and ever closer to the first ever brand new car. As I have mentioned before, this house was our first house with a steep driveway (our 'on belay' house). At the top of this driveway, in the garage, sat that first ever brand new car. Perhaps you've figured out already the story I am about to tell. In one swift motion, young son Kyle, with whom I had just shared a bonding Father's Day bike ride speedily and aggressively swept down the sidewalk, up the driveway, and into the garage….and into the first ever brand new car! His left handlebar met the right rear quarter panel with a long and sickening s-c-r-e-e-e-e-e-c-h! A s-c-r-a-a-a-a-a-a-t-c-h of equal length was quickly and indelibly etched into that perfect paint on that first ever brand new car.

    I did, then, two things correctly.

    First, I counted to ten s l o w l y.

    Then, with a smile on my face and true patience in my soul, I looked directly into Kyle's eyes and said, "Well, now we have something to remember this great day by."

    One other story of my developing verbal potential:

One of our most successful American airlines is Southwest. Low fares. Friendly service. Many cities. Online check in. The list goes on. Unfortunately, back in the day, the whole cattle call boarding process left a little to be desired. You may remember this. Rather than getting assigned a specific seat on the plane, a Southwest ticket holder would get a boarding pass with either A, B, or C printed on it. If you were fortunate enough to get an A ticket, you could board the plane first. (Or, as I often did, I would bend my leg up in my pants, attach a fake peg leg, borrow two or three kids in strollers, carry my guitar and a white cane, wear hearing aids, and commandeer the nearest wheelchair just in order to be a part of the pre-boarding clan. That usually worked pretty well, but only if I were in the B or C ticket group.) As you can imagine, I've seen it all in that crazy Southwest 'line' or 'series of lines' that all seem to elbow poke each other for leverage and dastardly jockeying for the top spot. I've seen people run, skip, hop, cut, maim, dismember, and even murder in order to get one or two places in front of everyone else. I even had one person say, "If you don't like the way they do it here, then go fly American." (Ironic.)

The biggest dispute was usually the 'what constitutes being in line?' question. The official position of Southwest Airlines is that the line begins with the people *standing*. However, it is very clear, that when people are sitting in the chairs provided, extending outward from the A sign or B sign or C sign, that they are clearly and rightfully in place. It's just common courtesy.

So I was waiting in the Southwest line, sitting in Seat #5, when this guy roughly passed over me and those sitting in Seats #1, #2, #3, and #4. He allied himself intimately with the A sign and stood smugly above the rest of the waiting passengers—three of whom were elderly women. (At times like these, I fantasize about having two or three screaming babies, because with open seating, such criers could be placed strategically behind said line-cutter for a good three or four hour flight!)

The man in Seat #2 respectfully and articulately confronted our friend (who was a doormat salesman from New York) about his audacity. Doormat Salesman From New York then launched into a beautiful and cogent diatribe on the 'rules' of Southwest. He let us all know that he was abiding by the rules, that what he was doing was correct, and he had every right to stand in the front of the line, regardless of what any of us thought or felt. Doormat Salesman From New York was rude, condescending, selfish, and obnoxious. (Other than that, he was a pretty cool guy.) After about six or seven minutes of arguing and discussing, I felt the urge to step in. I stood and slowly walked past Seats #4,3,2,1. Standing before Doormat Salesman From New York, I most calmly and firmly said, "Sir, with respect, there is 'right,' and there is 'polite.'"

Silence prevailed over our gate, all Southwest gates, American gates, United gates, Continental gates, and all other gates around the world. For a brief moment, all global aeronautic activity ceased. For with ten short words I was a part of unraveling one of the greatest riddles facing all aviation experts—solving once and for all the Great Southwest Seating Conundrum, as evidenced by the Doormat Salesman From New York's subsequent personal decision to humbly and willingly find his way back past Seats #1,2,3,4, and 5 to his rightful holding pattern in Seat #6.

We've been given words and language and syntax and vernacular and tone and volume and diction and grammar and timing and colloquialisms and slang and tempo and pitch and hyperbole and humor and sarcasm and blurts and phrases and sentences and soliloquies and monologues and recitations and quips and quickness as gifts to be engaged. Fortunately, we've also been given brains. For all of us, I think it's best to juxtapose the former with the latter—knowing when and how to most fully utilize the resource of speech. Much pain would be alleviated, and much good could be accomplished in this way.

13
My Heart is Heavy

From somewhere deep within me, I experience empathy and compassion. I don't know how they got there, but in the most intimate parts of my soul, there they are. It may seem incongruent to some, as it certainly does to me, that as selfish as I am on the outside, there is an equal or greater amount of care on the inside.

I call it 'The Man With Two Hearts' Syndrome. I wrote this little poem about someone else, but maybe there are Two Men with Two Hearts Each.

The Man With Two Hearts is a man I know well
And you'll know him, too, by this story I tell.
Upon its completion you may know what is true
Concerning the hearts that reside within you.

Heart One is protected—it's bitter and mad
It replays lifelong tapes that are sorry and sad.
It's broken, no doubt, and leaves no room for giving
And it barely can muster a reason for living.

You know how I know this? It shows on his face
For I've gone for a visit to this bitter man's place.
He sits in his La-Z-Boy morning 'til night
And the big screen before him does not leave his sight.

His biases rise as he clicks through the news
He denigrates liberals, gays, and Jews
He hates everyone not as perfect as he
Heart One is hurting and as dark as can be.

Through zillions of channels he's surfing at will
The cable ensures that he will get his fill
Of sensational, carnal, ugly, and violent
But then for a moment his remote becomes silent.

For a story has captured his sudden attention
And melting away are his anger and tension
For there on the screen is an uncommon report
About children called 'special' and their special sport.

The kids are competing, try as they might
It's called the Olympics, but something's not right
Their limbs are all contorted, the cadence offbeat
Their sweet smiles are crooked, they're slow on their feet.

I pause for a moment and then take a chance
Giving The Man With Two Hearts a quick glance
And what to my curious gaze should appear
But a glimpse of his eyes and they're brimming with tears

I feel my heart race as the hope rises in me
For I've witnessed a wonder I've not expected to see.
The man with Heart One—the one black through and through
Has but for a second engaged Heart Number Two.

Heart Two is a heart that is filled with compassion
That looks at the needy and moves us to action
And now could it be that Heart Two will come through?
What good could this gifted man put himself to?

But as fast as it spikes, my hope quickly decreases
As the channel is changed opportunity ceases
The eyes once with tears are again concentrated
Focused on all that deserves to be hated.

I don't stand in judgment of The Man With Two Hearts

When it's all said and done, we're not that far apart.
For I'm constantly choosing the place that I'll live
Am I hoarding and careful, or willing to give?

Acknowledge the presence of ugly Heart One
And then, in so doing, sense the process begun
For brokenness won't have to paralyze you
But it can propel you to live by Heart Two

My Heart Number Two is ever-present, but there are three types of circumstances which most certainly kick it into high gear.

The first is what I call Little Guy Experiences. These are the Rocky-Hoosier-Rudy-Seabiscuit-Cinderella Team unexpected, come-from-behind, tears-welling-up inspiring stories that make you think that even you might have a chance!

This is why I love teachers.

This is why I love some pastors.

This is why I love good coaches.

This is why I love choir directors and team moms and Cub Scout leaders and big brothers and seniors-who-look-out-for-freshmen, and youth workers and big sisters and grandpas and grandmas and many managers at McDonald's and workers at homes for troubled kids and stress camp leaders and therapists and drug-alcohol counselors and just about anyone who will *let just about anyone come and get better and grow and win!* With the right leadership and the right timing and the right touch of even just a little luck, all those who were nobody become somebody. My hat is off to those who believe in the unbelievable, who accept the unacceptable, who mold the rigid—those who give of themselves to help others succeed in ways that most would never imagine. I have great hope for the hopeless when these people are at their finest.

My heart also goes out to people who find themselves involved in Unfortunate Situations, like my oldest son, Dex, when he was a first grader many years ago. As you may remember, we had just moved to the upper reaches of the Rocky Mountains in Colorado. Since we were way out in the boonies, Dex had to get to school some ten miles north and 1500' down. It was the middle of the school year and Mom and I decided that since he was now a first grader it was a good time for him to 'man up' and ride the bus. I mean, what was the worst that could happen, right?

Yeah. OK. Good one, folks.

We didn't find out about this until after the fact, which kind of bummed us out, thinking about how bummed out Dex must have been, but here's the report we got:

After receiving the parental pats on the snowy head and behind, he stepped up the gargantuan first step of that big yellow school bus. (By the way, 'yellow blue bus' is the phonetic rendering of 'I love you' in Russian—have I told you that?) But this had no blue. Just yellow with a black stripe. Then, up he stepped the second humungous big yellow with a black stripe school bus step, and then the third and fourth. The next moment has just got to be the worst possible experience for a new-kid-on-the-block-getting-on-the-bus-for-the-first-time: He turned left. Unless you are a psychotic pathological no-heart, you are feeling this big time right now. He turned left and faced the new kids. Ugh. Then, he began to step slowly, slowly by each row of seats as each terrorist-pagan-snot-nosed-brat-slimeball (maybe that's a little strong) rejected, shunned, humiliated, and otherwise did not welcome Dex Ballard. Slowly, slowly, slowly, he moved toward the back of the bus—with sneers and spit wads and noogies and physical assaults and verbal taunts (maybe that's a little strong) accompanied every painful step.

Then, the moment of all hell bus moments: the crackle of the bus PA, followed the voice of God Himself, "Dex Ballard…Sit down!'

That's when Dex snapped! And I'm so proud of him because he walked back up the front of the aisle, climbed over the bus driver barrier, commandeered that bus and drove it the ten miles down the hill to school. (And he was only six!) When he got there he yelled authoritatively, "All of you off the bus! And never again will I stand for such derisiveness! Now off, all of you! And even the sixth graders submitted. Then Dex turned to the bus driver himself and said, "I hereby remand you to the custody of the bus garage and the authorities therein. You are suspended until further notice, because never again will a young child be permanently damaged by your insensitivity!"

Again, I am quite proud, and I'm looking forward to the Made For TV movie.

The other times when my 'heart goes out,' are those moments of crisis when I find myself in the position of 'first responder.'

I really have to probe this, though, as I think that it might be my craving of adrenaline that makes me hyper-activate in crisis situations.

Several years ago, Frayne suggested that we all go to the California State Fair.

Pause.

I asked, "Are there people there?"

Pause.

I asked, "Do you really want to go?"

Pause.

I asked, "Am I correct in assuming that since this is a family event, you would like me to go?"

Let me just say that I would rather lick slimy goo off of the underside of a septic truck than go to any kind of State Fair or other event where there are hot, sticky, noisy, profane, pushy, hot-dog-filled, beer-drunk, loudmouth on-the-verge-of-puking Merry-Go-Round and Ferris Wheel riders. (Pretty neighborly of me, ain't it?)

It only took us forty five minutes to get there.

But, the good news is that we got there early. ('Early to fair, early to leave, makes a man healthy, wealthy, and a survivor,' that's what I always say.)

We pulled off the main road into the driveway of the parking lot about three days before the gates opened. We were, quite surprisingly, the first car there. We turned again and headed toward the lot fee collection booths. There were about eight of them abreast, but only two in the middle were open. I headed for the one on the right. And felt the strangest sensation. It wasn't that I saw anything. It's that I felt something. Only later could I put the pieces together, the almost simultaneous white flash, wife's gasp and words, "Oh my gosh, he hit that man!"

A white 15-passenger van (driven by a police officer and filled with inmates) was going very speedily out the in! An elderly booth attendant stepped off of the sidewalk, and the side view mirror of the whizzing van knocked him off his feet and into the middle of the roadway! I leapt from our vehicle, ran across the driveway, and knelt by the man's side. He was moaning in pain, so I simply cradled him in my arms and prayed for him—encouraging him all the while. (Dumbhead police guy was beyond delusional—asserting his innocence by saying he was driving the speed limit!) I could feel every empathetic energy within me find its way from heart and soul toward this poor old guy who was victimized so dramatically and unjustly by a person who should have least hurt him.

Jimmy Chavez, my new 70-year-old friend, quickly and fully recuperated from his injuries, and continues to send me Christmas cards.

So, all of these memories keep coming up—the lady who hit the pine tree after spinning out on rain-slickened 172nd, the lady who drowned right before our eyes at Hanauma Bay, the cyclist on Murray whose chain locked up and sent him flying, the man in the Chicago restaurant that collapsed to the floor in a sudden seizure…

My heart goes out to them. And my heart goes out to you, when you struggle and suffer and feel desperate and hopeless.

And I don't think it's just the adrenalin thing, for I've been there a time or two myself.

14
My Bible is Dusty

I told you at the beginning that I'm a Christian—or as some of us have been saying lately, a Christ follower. Actually, I think Christ Participator is most accurate for me. If you're still reading, then you are apparently okay with that. Or maybe, I come across different than some of the other Christ Participators you have read or talked to or been hit over the head by.

Some would say that I'm not a very good Christ Participator. Others think I'm a better Christian than I really probably am.

I don't know if there's such a thing as a good Christ Participator or a bad Christ Participator

A Christ Participator just is.

If I say the f-word when I really, really lose my temper, does that make me a bad Christ Participator? (Is it worse that I say the f-word or that I lose my temper?)

If I give $200 to a guy who is doing something good in the world, does that make me a good Christ Participator? (Is it better if that $200 made things a little tighter for me at the end of the month than if it was leftover 'gig' money that might just have easily been given to my kid swimmers who happen to have good aim?)

If I'm greedy or egocentric or lustful or desperate or selfish or rude or loud mouthed or angry, am I any less of a Christ Participator than when I'm playing or singing or preaching or wedding-and-funeral-officiating or shaking hands at the exit door of the church?

I'm not too sure about these things.

When I 'accepted the Lord Jesus Christ as my personal Savior' and 'asked him into my heart', (ohmygosh, what a weird bunch of words all strung together), I was nine years old, a fourth-grader experiencing inexplicable wonder and jumping up and down on the top bunk of his bed with joy—the emotion, not the girl. The old hymn says, "Floods of joy o'er my soul like the sea billows rolled, since Jesus came into my heart," not that I ever, ever allow myself to sing that song anymore.

When I was a 20-something seminary student, I just as easily could say, "You know, this seems like an awful lot of bullshit to me." Not sure when I was really the 'better' Christ Participator, age nine or age 20-something. Not sure if I was a better Christ Participator receiving what Mom handed to me or doing my very best to apostacize myself and reject the whole thing altogether.

My road to and through Christ Participation (Christianity) is a winding one with lots of dark trees and weird turns in the way. It began Episcopalian, then non-denominational, then Evangelical Free (some would say this title is a contradiction in terms), then ELCA (one of the more 'liberal' Lutheran branches), then AG (of the Swaggart and Bakker ilk), then Foursquare (still don't know what that means, except it has a big red rubber ball included—not meaning to be irreverent here), and then Conservative Baptist. Mixed into these events were a couple of 'para-church' organizations during my youth and college years.

Gosh, that brings up a random memory! I was part of this thing called Youth Dynamics during my freshman and sophomore years. It was fun, and there were people there that cared about me. I remember a guy named Chuck, but that's about it. Chuck. Hmmm. I remember he took me on a ride in a car the first time I ever got together with him, and I thought it would never end. I almost fell asleep with my head against the window, but I remember feeling bad about that, because Chuck was really trying to care for me. But, I must have appreciated him for that, because I started singing in a Youth Dynamics singing group. The memory that comes, is when I went to one of the rehearsals, and I was wearing a green polyester running jacket with yellow stripes, and I had the cuffs pulled up to the elbows, (because I liked feeling the veins on my arms because that made me feel muscular when I wasn't), and this girl asked me, "Do you have toilet paper stuffed up in your shirt to make you look like you have big biceps?" That was kind of a weird question. I said, "No, but I did stuff some down the front of my pants." That surprised her a lot, and I don't know if I ever remember her asking me another question again ever, or anyone else for that matter.

After all of that, I ended up at a church camp run by the Evangelical Covenant Church, (which majors on the majors and minors on the minors, and, of course, the biggest major to some is what is a major and what is a minor.) And that is where I met my wife and got locked into vocational ministry and got my licensing done and got commissioned, which means I'm practically ordained, except I don't really care to be, because of all the political requirements that bug me and bring out my cynical and rebellious side.

So, back to the 'am I a good Christ Participator' question…maybe it's better to ask if I'm a 'good minister.'

Uh. Hmmm. Maybe.

What I don't do: Steal money. Sleep around. Wield power like a sword. (Those are the Big Three.) I don't preach too long. I'm not generally disingenuous. I don't say one thing and do another. (The Medium Three.) I like being looked at. I like being laughed at for the right reasons. I have a hard time with the Bible. (The Little Two and the other Really Big One, I guess.)

This is funny, because I'm a pastor in a B-I-B-L-E church. (Yes, that's the book for me. I stand alone on the Word of God, the B-I-B-L-E, we sang unabashedly as 9-year-olds.) Some people are a little concerned about me in this regard, as they see the Bible as wonderful and amazing. I still can't not see it as impossible…but I'm at least reading it again and pretty excited to get to the parts where the Red Sea gets parted and then the Jordan and then Jericho gets leveled by, of all things, trumpets and shouts.

All in all, I want to do and be everything perfect, that's for sure. I want to get up early and read my dusty Bible for all it's worth, while I listen to the drip-drop of the rain on the porch, sipping the coffee or tea in the emerging dawn light, and pray and write down thoughts in The Burgundy Brain II, and smile when my family rises, and eat oatmeal and wheat toast and pet Sierra at my feet.

I want to laugh with my friends, ski on glass, climb figurative and literal mountains, learn all I can, and attempt to negotiate the difficulty of people who want to do me harm.

I really want to exercise intensely and get rock hard abs and calves of steel and pecs that flex and hair on my head, (well, only so much is in my control), and feel good physically without the blown knees and bulging discs and plantar fascia issues.

I want to drive to work without caring too much about getting there first and maybe smile at people on the way.

I want to treat my coworkers and colleagues with dignity and respect and have fun with them and laugh a whole bunch and learn together how to lay down our lives for the sake of the redemption and beautification of a lost and hopeless world, and then celebrate with them when we see some successes here and there.

I want to come home with a smile on my face and look deeply into the eyes of my wife and children—to really pay attention to how and what they feel, to play Monopoly and Pinochle, and enjoy evenings of their loving intimacy.

I really want to sleep peacefully with a balanced excitement about waking up the next morning.

I want to put into practice what the dusty Bible says—to be thankful always, to love others more than myself, and to pay good attention to the giving God that I have come to believe in.

I hope that I can be the type of person that can translate these dreams, opportunities, gifts, and recognitions into some kind of communicative form that will help you achieve whatever it is you are hoping.

I really look forward to having lots of good and memorable and worthy material for the next little bit of writing.

That would just make my day.

www.ingramcontent.com/pod-product-compliance
Lightning Source LLC
LaVergne TN
LVHW011427080426
835512LV00005B/302